Patrick Ness has lived in Hawaii, California and Washington state. He moved to London in 1999. He is the author of one novel, *The Crash of Hennington*, reviews books for the *Daily Telegraph*, and has won a London Writers' Prize for his short fiction.

By the same author

The Crash of Hennington

Topics About Which I Know Nothing

patrick ness

HARPER PERENNIAL

Harper Perennial
An imprint of HarperCollins*Publishers*
77–85 Fulham Palace Road
Hammersmith, London W6 8JB

www.harpercollins.co.uk/harperperennial

This edition published by Harper Perennial 2005

First published by Flamingo 2004

Two of the stories in this collection have previously appeared in the
following publications:
'Sydney is a City of Jaywalkers' in *Genre* magazine © Patrick Ness 1997;
and 'The Way All Trends Do' in *Ambit* © Patrick Ness 2000

Patrick Ness asserts the moral right to be identified
as the author of this work

A catalogue record for this book is available from the British Library

ISBN 978-0-00-713944-6

Set in Sabon by Palimpsest Book Production Limited, Polmont, Stirlingshire

Printed and bound in Great Britain by Clays Ltd, St Ives plc

For Vicki Burrows, Belle of Puyallup

We've got so many tchotchkes,
We've practically emptied the Louvre.
In most of our palaces,
There's hardly room to manoeuvre.
Well, I shan't go to Bali today,
I must stay home and Hoovre
Up the gold dust.

That doesn't mean we're in love.

The Magnetic Fields

Contents

implied violence

1

'Implied violence,' says the boss, 'is our bread and butter.'

He means implied violence is what we sell, which it isn't, we sell self-defence courses over the phone, but the boss likes to think in themes. He's talking to the new girl, Tammy, which sounds American to me. I'll have to ask Percy.

'I don't like to say we need to frighten our customers,' says the boss, looking down at Tammy who is looking right back up at the boss, 'but let me put it this way: we need to frighten our customers.' This makes the boss laugh. Tammy laughs as well, too loud and too long. I look over to Maryam from Africa who meets my gaze.

There are only three of us, now four, who work in this little room, but we all wear nametags. Mine says my name, Maryam from Africa's says hers, and Percy's says his, but I notice that Tammy's says 'Terrific Tammy'. I look back at Maryam. She's noticed it, too. She rolls her eyes as Tammy's laugh just goes on and on.

2

On one side of me sits Percy. Percy is a very large bloke who falls over a lot. 'I have an inner-ear problem,' he says. Percy calls himself my mate.

On the other side of me is Maryam from Africa. Maryam from Africa is from Africa. I'm not sure which part, because I didn't think you were supposed to ask. I'm not sure how to pronounce her name exactly either, because she says it in her accent and you can't really ask her to repeat it. She frowns all the time but is not a mean person and doesn't mind, I don't think, that I just call her Maryam. She must be about fifty or so, but I wouldn't be surprised at anything in a twenty-five-year range above or below that.

The three of us sit in a line facing one wall of our room, Maryam by the door, me, then Percy by the window. It's one long desk with a computer, telephone and headset for each of us, but dividers separate us so we can have privacy to talk to potential customers. Behind us, there used to be only a wall, but now they've put Tammy at a card table against it. There isn't very much room, so Tammy's facing the window, and our backs are facing her side.

Why did they put her in here? There's only room for three.

'There's only room for three,' whispers Percy, but he has to lean towards me to do this and he falls off his stool. 'I have an inner-ear problem,' he says to Tammy and the boss, standing back up. 'It affects my balance.'

3

'Everyone here has a sales quota,' says the boss. 'It's not a bad one, not a very high one, but it's important that you meet it each week.'

Tammy nods. I don't like the way she nods.

'Because if you don't,' the boss puts his face close to Tammy's, 'we'll have to send you to the end of the hall.'

Tammy laughs. No one else does. The boss smiles, but it's not a laughing kind of smile.

'And what's at the end of the hall?' says Tammy, still thinking it's all for fun.

'Only people who don't meet their quota ever find out,' says the boss.

'And no one's returned to tell the tale?' Still smiling, still laughing.

'I'm sure you'll meet your quota just fine.'

Tammy's forehead wrinkles a bit at how seriously the boss says this. She opens her mouth again but then closes it.

'You've already met your colleagues, yes?' The boss gestures towards the three of us on this side of the room. We all nod.

'They introduced themselves this morning when I came in,' says Tammy.

That was only because we were discussing why there was a card table with a new computer, a new phone and a new headset crammed in the corner where Percy used to slide his chair back when he needed a few minutes' break. In walked Tammy. The room was too small not to say hello.

'Boss?' says Percy.

'Yes, Percival,' says the boss.

('Everyone calls me Percy,' Percy said to Tammy this morning.)

'I'm wondering if Tammy's going to be, you know, comfortable.'

'Comfortable?' says the boss.

'Yeah, in that small corner, like,' says Percy, looking at the floor, scratching the back of his neck. 'It's usually three to a room, isn't it?'

'Yes, Percival, you're correct,' says the boss, still with the not-laughing kind of smile. 'It is usually three to a room, but just now we haven't an extra space to slot Tammy in.'

'All the other rooms are full?'

'All the other rooms are full.'

'No one's gone to the end of the hall lately,' says Tammy, already trying to make a joke. No one laughs. Tammy doesn't notice.

'It's only temporary, Percival,' says the boss. 'I trust you'll make our newest sales representative as comfortable as your colleagues made you on your arrival.'

Maryam and I ignored Percy for a week. He replaced Karen, who had gone to the end of the hall. We hadn't really liked her, but we were surprised she hadn't met quota. It really isn't a very high quota.

'Of course, boss,' says Percy.

'Good,' says the boss. 'If you have any questions, Tammy, I'm sure these three will be more than happy to help. I'll let you all get to work.' He leaves without looking at anyone. Maryam from Africa gives a 'hmph' to the whole thing.

4

'What you have to consider,' I say into my headset, 'is what would a woman like yourself do if an intruder broke in one night when you were on your own with the children?'

'I'd call Emergency Services.'

'What if he cut the phone lines?'

'I'd let my rottweiler do what rottweilers do.'

'What if he'd brought minced beef with poison in it to put your rottweiler out of commission?'

'He's very persistent, this intruder.'

'They always are, madam. I assure you, it's not a laughing matter.'

'I'd spray him with mace.'

'You've left it in the car.'

'I don't have a car.'

'You've left it at your friend's house when you were showing her how to work it.'

'I'd scream.'

'He's taped your mouth while you slept.'

'After he poisoned my rottweiler and cut the phone lines.'

'There's been a rash of similar crimes in your area, ma'am. I'm only reporting the facts.'

'Do you even know my area?'

I check the list. There's no town name, but luckily I recognise the dialling code.

'Derby, madam.'

'Listen, this horror show has been very amusing, but I really must –'

'What if he went for your children first and made you watch?'

'That's not funny.'

'As I've said, madam, it never is. We offer self-defence training for the entire family.'

'My daughter is five.'

'Never too young to learn where to kick.'

'It'd frighten the life out of her.'

'I beg to differ, madam. Knowing a few basic moves might boost her confidence right at the time she's about to enter school. Think about bullies, madam.'

'*Five*, for pity's sake.'

'Most karate black belts start at three, madam.'

'You're making that up.'

I am. 'I assure you I'm not, madam. One of the major positive points that clients have told us is that the self-defence classes have given them the *appearance* of confidence, and over 90 per cent have never even been forced to use their training.'

'And that's a selling point, is it?'

'An armed world is a safe world, madam.'

'I suppose so . . .'

'Why not make your world a little safer, madam? Why not do yourself and your daughter, no matter how young, the service of being able to face the world with one more resource?'

'Anything to help me sleep at night, is that right?'

'That's right, madam. Couldn't have said it better myself.'

5

'So what exactly is at the end of the hall?' says Tammy.

We're eating our lunches. The company doesn't have a canteen, so we have to eat at our desks. I have a cheddar and ham sandwich that I make five of on a Sunday. By the smell of it, Maryam from Africa has a cold curry. Percy seems to have just pickles. His wife sometimes forgets to go shopping, he says. Tammy has gone outside to the sandwich shop down on the corner and got herself some kind of leafy salad and a fruit drink. We spend all our mornings talking on the phone, so lunch is usually a quiet affair. Not for Tammy, apparently.

'It is what the boss says it is,' I say.

'All he said is that only people who don't meet quota know what it is,' says Tammy.

'Exactly,' I say.

'That doesn't make sense,' she says.

'It is what it is,' says Percy, who has to steady himself with one hand when he looks up to say this.

'Is it metaphorical, like?' asks Tammy.

'No, it's just down that way,' says Percy. He jerks his thumb in the right direction.

'I mean,' says Tammy, openly laughing at Percy, 'that it's just words the boss uses to motivate us. *Implied violence*. Like in our sales pitch.'

'No,' I say, 'it really is just down that way.'

'But that doesn't –'

'You meet your quota, then you never find out,' interrupts Maryam from Africa. Her accent is a hell of a thing, foreign and stern, like being shouted at by a vampire maid. 'Can we eat in silence, please? I hear enough chitter chatter all day long without having my digestion interrupted by nonsense of this sort.'

6

The self-defence classes we sell have no connection with this company. We're just the telesales firm that the self-defence people hired to push their product. I've never been to a class. I've never even seen a brochure. Neither have Maryam from Africa or Percy for all I know. So far, Tammy hasn't asked, and I'll bet it's the sort of thing she would ask about, so I'm guessing that maybe she's seen a brochure or been to a class. It would figure.

7

'Should we invite her to the pub?' says Percy.

'Who?' I ask, though who else could he be talking about?

'Tammy.'

'Good God, no,' whispers Maryam from Africa.

'It's rude not to,' says Percy.

'It's rude to ask questions all day,' says Maryam. 'If you invite her, I'm not coming.'

'You never come,' says Percy.

'I might today, if you don't invite her.'

We prepare ourselves for an awkward moment when the day ends, but Tammy just bags up the jumper she's slung over the back of her chair, waves bye, and leaves.

'The cheek,' says Maryam.

8

I bring two pints of bitter and one pint of lager to the table. The lager is for Maryam from Africa. It seems surprising that she drinks lager, but I suppose there's no reason she shouldn't. I get the drinks every night, even when it's just me and Percy, because Percy can't be trusted to carry anything. He's all right once he's standing or once he's sitting; it's the in-between that's tricky, and that includes leaning. The management of the Cock & Cloisters have even barred him from handling small glasses of spirits.

'Cheers, mate,' says Percy. Maryam from Africa nods a thank you. Percy and I each take a swig from our bitters. Maryam downs half of her pint in one long, graceful draught. It's almost beautiful. She dabs her lip with a serviette and says, 'I don't like this new girl.'

'Me neither,' I say.

'She's not so bad,' says Percy.

'You say that about everyone,' I say.

'You say the boss isn't so bad,' says Maryam.

'He isn't,' says Percy.

Maryam looks at me with eyebrows that say 'point proven'.

'And what kind of a name is Tammy for a grown woman?' she says.

'I reckon it's American,' I say, 'but she doesn't sound American.'

'It's South African,' says Percy. 'Short for Tamara.'

We stare at him.

'How d'you know that?' asks Maryam.

'I asked,' says Percy.

'When?' I say.

'On the afternoon break,' he says. 'You were in the loo. Maryam was on the phone to her mum. It was just me and Tammy, so I asked. Polite conversation.'

Maryam hmphs again.

'Hi everyone,' says Tammy, suddenly appearing at our table from the cigarette haze of the pub.

'You left before we could ask you along,' says Percy, fast, before the rest of us even take in who Tammy is.

'That's all right,' says Tammy. 'I'd agreed to meet the boss here anyway.' She points towards the bar, and sure enough, there's the boss holding what looks like a pint of Guinness and a G & T. Maryam from Africa sighs and starts scooting over to make room for Tammy and the boss.

'No need,' says Tammy. 'We're sitting over there with some of the workers from the other rooms. What am I saying? I'm sure you know them better than I do.'

We all look to the corner she's pointing at. From the

silence, I gather I'm not the only one who doesn't recognise anyone.

'Every room is kind of its own little world,' says Percy.

'Of three people?' says Tammy hysterically. Is she on drugs that she's this upbeat? 'Awfully small world, if you ask me.' She punches Percy playfully on the shoulder. He falls off his chair to the green, sticky carpet. 'Oh my God,' says Tammy. 'I'm so sorry.'

'Nothing to worry about,' says Percy, helping himself back up. 'You weren't to know.'

We all hear the boss say Tammy's name across the pub. He still has the drinks. He sees us, but he doesn't come over. That's the way everyone wants it.

'Gotta go,' says Tammy. 'See you all tomorrow.'

'I hope she doesn't have any problem meeting her quota,' says Percy, watching the back of Tammy move away from us.

'She won't,' says Maryam from Africa. 'Probably get the quota *raised*, her.'

'And you're married, Perce,' I say.

'It doesn't mean my eye is wandering if I hope that someone doesn't get sent to the end of the hall,' he says.

'Never gonna happen,' says Maryam, before downing the rest of her pint. It's even more beautiful when she does it this time.

9

'I don't mean to alarm you, madam,' I say, 'but it's a fact that crime rates for Hove are through the roof this year.'

'Uh-huh.'

'With our self-defence course, though, that fact doesn't have to scare you.'

'Uh-huh.'

'In fact, it's not self-defence we're selling. It's peace of mind.'

'You've said *fact* three times in a row.'

'I believe in the product, madam.'

'How much are you asking for it?'

'Can you really put a price tag on peace of mind?'

'*You* obviously have.'

10

Today Tammy's nametag says 'Tammy On Top.' I hear her talking to a customer on the phone behind me.

'Listen, Mrs Rosen,' she says, '*I* got your phone number, didn't I? Ex-directory is only a lie that keeps you from getting called by those too lazy to do further searching.'

We're given a list of phone numbers to call every day generated by some marketing firm somewhere. It isn't supposed to have any ex-directory numbers on it. Mine doesn't.

'And if *I* can get it, think how much more information

the malevolent criminal mind is going to find out about you, Mrs Rosen. You. He's going to come after you, and he's going to know a lot more about you than your phone number, I can tell you that. He's going to know when you're alone; when you're in your nightgown; when you make your evening cup of tea and sit down to *The Times* crossword. He's going to break into your house silently. He's going to take your phone off the hook. He's going to come up behind you, and then he's going to silence you. But he's not going to knock you out, Mrs Rosen. Oh, no, he's got better ideas than that. He's going to keep you awake, because before he robs you, he's . . . well, I hesitate to even suggest. I'd hate to give you nightmares.'

In less than another minute, she's got Mrs Rosen, no doubt a widowed pensioner because that's today's target audience, to sign up for the top-of-the-line classes which include advanced jujitsu, proper use of a knife, and night-time camouflage, all for more than what Mrs Rosen will spend on food in a year.

Jesus *dammit*.

11

There's a sheet up on the wall that lists our quotas for the week and our progress towards them. We each write our daily sales numbers in a box beside our name and underneath the day. Tammy's only been here since Wednesday. It's Friday morning. She's already outsold Percy and is only three behind me. The second-to-last sale I made yesterday made me reach weekly quota.

Percy has to sell four more to make it, no problem really, but none of us can believe that Tammy will probably make a full week's quota without even needing to. Tammy is in a meeting with the boss. A new employee thing, we all assume, probably accompanied by many smiles and laughs if Tammy's performance on the quota sheet is anything to go by.

'It's because she's new,' says Maryam from Africa.

'Aye,' I say.

'All that enthusiasm for the product in the first couple of days,' says Percy.

'It'll wear off,' says Maryam.

The company only gives Maryam from Africa the numbers of African women her own age, and her sales are so far beyond mine and Percy's that her quota is higher. She passed it Wednesday morning, but she'll only report passing it this afternoon. If they knew she'd passed it so easily, they'd raise it again, and it's already twice the usual. She takes it easy the rest of the week, a sale here, a sale there. I'd do the same.

Tammy appears suddenly, in the way that we're already trying to get used to, and I notice that the three of us act like guilty children getting caught doing nothing. Her nametag says 'Tammy Triumphant'. She still has that stupid smile on her face, but she seems distracted by something.

'There's some kind of disturbance at the end of the hall,' she says. She walks to her seat, almost talking to herself. 'The boss ended the meeting to go handle it.' We realise she's angry. 'He wouldn't let me come down and see.' She puts on her headset, already dialling the number at the top of the list. Percy, Maryam and I look at one another. We listen for sounds from the end of the hall but hear nothing. Maryam reaches over from her seat to shut the door.

Tammy's phone picks up. 'I know you're alone, Mrs Wilson,' she says.

12

Ten minutes later, the boss comes in.

'Stay in your office,' he says. His face is set, worried. 'Don't leave, no matter what you hear.'

'What's going on?' says Percy.

'Just stay here,' he says. He looks over at Tammy. She holds his eye for a moment, then raises her eyebrows before looking back to her computer. The boss closes the door behind him. Percy looks at me.

'What's going on?' he says again.

'How should I know?' I say.

'Best to leave it,' says Maryam from Africa.

'What do you mean *Best to leave it*?' Tammy says, spinning round to face us.

Maryam's posture straightens. It suddenly looks like she's a whole lot bigger.

'Exactly what I say, Little Madam,' she says. 'Best. To. Leave. It. Get back to work.' She looks at Percy. 'Some of us have quotas to meet.' Percy turns back to his terminal and starts dialling the next number.

'Aren't any of you curious?' says Tammy, looking at us, exasperated. 'They tell you to avoid the end of the hall, and you just say, *Fine by me*?'

I look at Maryam, who still has her eyes locked on Tammy. I look back at Tammy.

'It's not quite like that,' I say.

'Then what is it like?' Tammy says. 'What's wrong with you? Don't you want to know?'

'Well,' I say, 'the reality of it is –'

'Go look yourself if you're so interested, Miss Missy,' says Maryam.

'Maryam!' I say. Maryam looks at me.

'The woman is not going to be satisfied until she has a look,' Maryam says. 'She is just gathering her courage. Well, I say leave us be with your courage-gathering and just go if you're going to go.'

Tammy takes off her headset. She stands. 'All right then,' she says, 'I will.'

'Tammy,' I say, 'I really wouldn't.'

'And yet you can't, or won't, tell me why,' she says.

Percy is also trying to mouth at Tammy not to go, but he's on a call. It's company policy that you never disconnect a call. Percy over-balances and hits the floor with a thud. 'No, madam, I'm still here,' he says, waving his hands at Tammy to stay put.

'This is ridiculous,' Tammy says. She looks at each one of us in turn, then opens the door and steps out.

13

'I wish you wouldn't have let her go,' says Percy, finally through with his call. It was successful, leaving just three to go to make quota.

'There is no letting involved,' says Maryam. 'A person chooses their own actions. We chose to stay here. She chose to go.'

'She wouldn't have listened to us, Perce,' I say.

'I suppose not,' he says. 'But the end of the hall,' he says to himself, shaking his head as he starts dialling again.

14

Through the still-open door, we hear a distant scuffling, then something that might be a muted voice or it could be the air conditioning malfunctioning like it often does, then a faint crash, followed by a few more crashes, then an uncomfortable high-pitched sound, which again could be the air conditioning.

We all carry on with our calls. Maryam reaches out and closes the door.

15

Much later, the boss comes in. There is a cut across his cheek and a bandage peeking out from his shirt collar. He is walking with a limp, and there is a funny smell.

Without saying a word, he walks over to Tammy's table, folds up her jumper, puts it in her bag, picks it up and leaves. We watch him go. Percy looks at his watch.

'Where did the day go?' he says.

We get ready to leave, and one by one we enter today's sales numbers on the weekly quota sheet, first Maryam, then me, then Percy.

It takes us a minute to realise we've had our best day ever.

the way all trends do

Nabbed!
The Groomgrab[1] Phenomenon at the Turn of the Millennium

For fulfillment of the requirements of SOCI 917, 'Methodologies, Dichotomies, Paradoxes, Iconographics, and Uncomfortable Shoes: The Millennial Nonsense and Why Everyone Made Such a Big Deal Out of It Instead of Pretending It Was Just Another Stupid Year, Which It Was.' Professor Megan Woodhall/Sjoboen-Pimlico/Wren, Instructor, University of Western Los Angeles, Including Brentwood, Malibu, Santa Monica, and Scattered Portions of Ventura County
November 30, 2015

It seems to have begun the way all trends do, with whim meeting opportunity.

The first groomgrab[2], as they came to be

---

[1] In the interests of full disclosure, the author wishes to state that he was groomgrabbed at the age of nine. He was taken to the Glendale Galleria, outfitted in Ralph Lauren, and deposited back home with a chocolate-chip cookie and a copy of *World* magazine. Although he remembers the experience as 'delightful,' he wishes to express his intentions to remain objective on the matter.

[2] This paper will use the original lower-case spelling of the term commonly used in most Western U.S. media. The trend started in the West and was only (mistakenly) capitalized in an aggressively negative *Washington Times* editorial.

known[3], can be traced back to July 14, 1999 to an area of Los Angeles then known as Westwood. James Roddick, 28, gay, single, and Anton Marshall, 27, also gay, also single[4], were driving home from a movie when they spotted seven-year-old Aaron Booher playing ball by himself on the sidewalk. '"Desultory" was the word that came to mind,' Marshall is reported to have said. Some eleven weeks later, just when groomgrabs were on the upswing, Roddick and Marshall appeared on the *Sally Jessy Raphael Show* to describe that historic first occurrence.

> Roddick: [Booher] was just bouncing the ball, all by himself.
>
> Marshall: It was the saddest thing.
>
> Roddick: So Anton goes, 'Poor kid, doesn't look like he's having any fun at all.'
>
> Marshall: It was true, and you should have seen his clothes. I mean, who puts their kids outside in corduroy in July?
>
> Roddick: Or any month?
>
> Marshall: Really. Just because he's seven doesn't mean he doesn't notice what he's wearing.
>
> Roddick: Right. So I said, 'Someone should just grab him and take him to the Gap.'
>
> Marshall: Re-do him top to bottom.
>
> Roddick: Buy him an ice cream cone or a Mrs Field's.

---

[3] Distinct from the fabgrab, which evolved later.

[4] They were 'just friends.'

Marshall: Give him a nice time, in other words.

Sally Jessy: And that's when you –

Roddick: That's when we picked him up, yes.

Sally Jessy: You 'grabbed' him.

Marshall: Hence the name.

Three and a half hours later, Marshall and Roddick dropped Booher back on the same sidewalk, dressed in a new tan, short-sleeve, sueded crewneck sweater; khaki walking shorts; and a pair of Timberland Kids sandals. He also carried bags filled with Gap Kids polo shirts, a Guess Kids belt, a stuffed Godzilla, and a Richard Scarry book on multiples of five[5]. Booher's parents, Mr and Mrs Donald Booher, were unaware anything had happened until Aaron returned home. The police report includes the fact that Aaron repeatedly asked his mother, his father, the police officer, anyone he could find: 'Can I go again tomorrow?'

All arguments and counter-arguments to the practice of the 'groomgrab' begin here with little Aaron Booher's question. 'You see,' say the grabbers, 'Booher was never in danger and had a little fun injected into his life for the first time in ages.' Anti-grabbers, with some merit, point out that seven year olds also often find activities like

---

[5] Which may or may not have been appropriate to Booher's age, but neither Roddick nor Marshall had nieces or nephews by which to gauge when a child would have read a certain book. Marshall apparently had to talk Roddick out of Judy Blume.

vomiting and bee-stomping fun, i.e. a seven year old
is not exactly the best judge of what good, healthy
entertainment is. However, the point of this paper
is not to judge the action[6], merely to map its
movement across the country and see just how the
country got swept away in this most peculiar of
fads.

Witness Marcy 'Pebbles' Morrison, youngest
granddaughter of (then) 9th Circuit Court Judge
Bosco Morrison[7]. The younger Morrison, in her
seminal *Take Your Hands Back On Me!*[8], the first real
study of groomgrabbing as a cultural phenomenon,
reports that 'my own, personal groomgrabbing was the
most exciting couple hours of my life to date.
Nothing else has come close. I would trade the best
sex I ever had for that time in my childhood. In a
heartbeat. It was the first time *any* adult had
treated me like a special little human, and for no
reason, just because I was *there*.'
Morrison goes overboard somewhat by calling her
groomgrabbing an experience of feeling unconditional

---

[6] Though again, in the interests of disclosure, the author wishes to
indicate that he wouldn't trade his groomgrab experience for pretty
much anything in the world.

[7] The senior Morrison, of course, being President O'Donnell's recent,
controversial appointee to the Supreme Court.

[8] As well as *Groomgrabbing: A Reflective Memoir*, *The Groomgrab
Guidebook* (softcover), *A Personal Oral History of My Life Leading Up
to and Following My Groomgrabbing* (two volumes, audio only), *The
Groomgrabbing Sonnet Cycle*, and *The Groomgrabbing Find-A-Word*,
by which time it was pretty much agreed she was flogging a dead
horse.

love[9], but you can see her point. A research survey by the University of Maine, New Hampshire, Vermont, Including Parts of Barbados and St Lucia conducted in 2003, roughly a year after the trend had died down, reported that the groomgrabbed children 'overwhelmingly' reported the grabbing as an unequivocally positive experience. Looking at the survey's raw data, 'overwhelming' is actually an understatement for once. Fully 99.58 per cent answered 'emphatically yes' when asked if they considered their groomgrabbing to have been a good experience[10]. A smaller, more recent study of groomgrabbed children conducted by sociologist Zorah Blandershot-Fields at the University of Hawaii, Hilo, reported not only the same almost-impossibly-high satisfaction rate as the UMNHVIPBSL study[11], but also

---

[9] 'Unlike most girls, I'm not looking for my father in a husband; I'm looking for my groomgrabbers, which sucks because they were gay.'

[10] Only three out of 714 respondents reported negative experiences: A boy in Rochester, New York, said that his groomgrabber's idea of fun was three hours of Monopoly, an idea of fun with which the boy did not concur. A girl in Humptulips, Washington, reported that her groomgrabbers declined to let her select the colors of her own clothes, citing their expertise in 'someone with autumn features,' an event which traumatized the girl to such an extent that she has only worn black (a winter color, apparently) since her grabbing. The last was a boy from Tucson, Arizona, who had an anaphylactic reaction to some roasted peanuts at a minor league baseball game, something which he does not blame on his groomgrabbers and about which he says, 'Up until that point I was having a great time.'

[11] 99.01 per cent, 110 positive responses out of 111. The lone negative response was from the autumn-featured girl who also manages to pop up in the only two other studies of groomgrabbing: the infamous Brookings survey now in its eleventh year of litigation, and a surface-

showed scholastic achievement including SAT and AP scores miles and miles above the national average[12]. Naturally, in addition to the scientific studies, the anecdotal evidence is voluminous[13].

Some excerpts:

- Ronald Laramie, Butte, Montana: 'I didn't even think there *were* any gay people in Butte, so getting groomgrabbed never really entered my mind. As far as I know, I was the only one in the whole state to be grabbed[14]. My grabbers were this older couple who'd apparently driven all the way down I-90 from Deer Lodge, which, my God, has like seven people so you can just imagine the kind of risk they were taking. I was ten, and they took me to one of those pizza-arcade places, Charlie Cheese or something[15]. They also bought me

---

skim report in *Us-People* that was more personality profiles along the 'Whatever happened to . . .?' line rather than in-depth analysis.

[12] Thirty-seven interviewees scored a perfect 1600 on their SATs. Average was 1571 (almost a thousand points over the national average of 592), and most students generally had a fistful of 5s on AP subjects as varied and esoteric as Bavarian German and Mathematical Paradoxes.

[13] Literally. Blandershot-Fields' interviews alone comprise seventeen volumes.

[14] Not true. A nine-year-old girl was grabbed in Helena in the summer of 2001, and an eleven-year-old girl was grabbed in Missoula in early 2002. Interestingly enough, the two girls were opposing point guards in the 2009 Montana State Girls' Basketball Championship Finals. Missoula won.

[15] Probably either Chas E. Cheese Pizza or Charlie's Cheesy Pizzeria, both of which, remarkably, had chain stores in Butte. The latter closed its doors in 2006 as a result of litigation by the former.

a boxed set of *The Chronicles of Narnia* and this great little black suit with an antique *Golden Girls* tie. It was a ton of fun, and I pretty much became a celebrity. They even asked me to be Grand Marshal of the Elk Parade, which is a big deal in Butte.'

- Jessica Mankiewicz, Encino, California: 'It happened when I was seven, and I remember it was near Halloween. My two guys were Harry and Reed. Reed was Asian, and Harry had wavy red hair. It's funny how clear it all still is. Anyway, they asked what I wanted to be for Halloween, so of course I say *Spidergirl* because that movie had just come out[16]. So what do these guys do? They take me to the *studio* to get outfitted! My guess is that one of them *had* to work at the studio, because otherwise how would we have gotten back there? But I got this kickass little Spidergirl suit made of the same rubber they used in the movie. It weighed like 35 pounds. I dragged and sweated my way through trick-or-treating, but how cool was I that year?'

- Savon Carmichael, Carson City, Nevada: 'I remember that I'd been kicked out yet again from my group of so-called friends. See, I was a fat little kid, and unfortunately I wasn't even that

---

[16] *Spidergirl Eternal*, Universal, 2001. Record domestic take of $997 million only recently surpassed by P. T. Anderson's *Equestrians Ho!*

funny which is pretty much the only thing that
saves you if you're a kid and you're fat.
Actually, my grabbers, who weren't even black,
said it's pretty much the same thing with being
gay. If you're a sissy, you better fucking be
funny, or you're going to get your ass kicked. My
grab was just the simplest thing, you know? They
bought me a sweater and a watch which I still
have, and I remember, of all things, this belt.
This really nice entwined leather belt that
didn't have holes in it, you could just hook the
little prong anywhere in the entwined leather. Do
you get my meaning? It didn't have holes in it.
So I didn't have to worry about making a new hole
or being too fat for a hole. I could just wear it
however. I can't tell you how much something like
that meant to me. I really believe that that
little belt was a catalyst for everything I've
achieved so far. Med school[17], my beautiful wife,
everything. I owe those two guys a lot.'

- Maggie Nakagama, Cadley, Georgia: 'From what I've
  been told, I guess I was the first recognized
  fabgrab[18]. My couple didn't buy me any clothes,
  which is what I guess happened on the groomgrabs.
  I remember I was playing by myself in my
  babysitter's front yard, and these guys drove up

---

[17] Carmichael was one of the 37 perfect SATs.
[18] A variation on the groomgrab which focused more on having a fun time than on getting better clothes. These were especially popular in the East.

and grabbed me. They left a Fendi[19], and we drove to Six Flags Over Augusta. I just had the best time in the world. We spent hours there, *hours*, going on all these rides that my parents would never let me do, eating cotton candy, playing those parkway games. I mean, I threw up twice, but it was all in good fun. And you know, when I got back, the Fendi was still in the yard. No one had even noticed. My grabbers let me keep the flag so I could prove that it happened.'

• Hunter Poulsbo, Redding, California: 'I guess I had kind of a weird grab. Mine took me to a mall and bought me a new outfit, but what I really wanted to do was figure out fractions. I was only nine, and I was having the damnedest time figuring them out. So when they asked me what I wanted to do next, I said, "Fractions." And we spent the rest of the afternoon in a booth at McDonald's doing fractions. I don't think I would have ever cracked them if it hadn't been for my grab.'

---

[19] Referring, of course, to the dark blue flag left at the scene of a groomgrab. It originated during a groomgrab in Erie, Pennsylvania, when a groomgrabber wanted to leave a note but had no paper. He left a dark blue Fendi scarf he was wearing tied to a chainlink fence near the site of the grabbing, assuming (correctly) that if the parents came out to check on their son, they would figure out what happened. It's also how the blue flags came to be known as 'Fendis' or 'Fenders.'

Working in Pairs

Most of the anecdotes mention the still-unexplained phenomenon that all groomgrabbers worked in pairs, never alone, and never more than two. It's possible that since the first groomgrab by James Roddick and Anton Marshall happened with just the two of them an unspoken tradition formed. There is also the possibility that the still-tenuous feeling surrounding homosexuals and children[20] added an extra note of caution to the grabbers, that is, two homosexuals together was somehow less questionable than one homosexual alone with a child[21]. Other theories include the 'Ostensible Parental Substitution Matrix Principle' by Dr Timothy Prong of the University of Nome, Et Al, whereby the grabbers subconsciously acted as mother/father figures as a sort of 'Ideal Parental Pair' to enhance the grabbee's feeling of comfort, thereby displacing the 'Actual Parental Dichometric Placement' in the something-or-other for the somesuch and so on[22]. There is also an interesting idea put forth by the Gay and Lesbian Association for Public Statements in which the pleasure of the experience for each member of the grabber-grabbee

---

[20] Though less so since the introduction of the Spark-Bailey Outvitro Harvesting technique.

[21] Yet another example of the incongruous bends of logic taken as the millennial swirl wrapped the country in holier-than-thou contests.

[22] Whatever. As Dr Shaniqua Jackson, head of UWLAIBMSMSPVC's own History, Sociology, Gender, Xenophobia, Misogyny, and French Studies Department says, 'There's a reason Dr Prong is in Nome.'

group is enhanced by sharing it with two others
rather than just one, the grabber being able to
share the joy of the child with the other grabber
and the child feeling as if he or she is being
selected by not just one adult but by two, making
the child feel all the more special.

There seems to be no consensus among the
grabbers either. Given the veil of anonymity that
descended shortly after the *Sally Jessy Raphael*
interview[23], there exist only nineteen verified
interviewed grabbers, all within the first two
months of the trend[24]. There is scarcely a mention
of the significance or even reason for working in
pairs. All grabbers seemed to act in unspoken
agreement or with subconscious purpose. An (August
29, 1999) interview in the *Chicago Sun Times* with a
grabbee known only as Colin contains the only

---

[23] Along with the pairing aspect, anonymity remains a second puzzlement
of the phenomenon. The author had intended to devote a section to
the topic, but what can you really say except a bunch of theoretical
hokum without one jot of fact? One day, one hopes that a grabber will
at the very least write a memoir, to be published posthumously even,
giving the world some insight into the mysteries that remain about
groomgrabbing.

[24] The vast percentage of information about groomgrabbing comes, of
course, from the grabbees themselves, who share an abundance of
self-confidence and media-savvy. An astonishing fourteen out of twenty-
five nominees of on-air personalities for last year's Talk Show Emmy
Awards were former grabbees. Average age: 24. Grabbees won all five
categories, including Trinity Sheffield-Conyers, 22, who won the coveted
Host of the Year, an award that had never previously gone to someone
under 40. This year, grabbees account for nineteen of the twenty-five
nominees with Sheffield-Conyers considered a lock to repeat as Host of
the Year.

mention this researcher could find in any of the published materials on grabbing[25]:

'At first, my lover and I just thought it was a neat idea. You know, sort of sprucing a kid up without any of the leftover responsibility. All of the good, none of the bad. Like being a grandparent for a day. But then it just sort of took on a life of its own. It was kind of an unspoken thing between the two of us that we never mentioned and that we never talked about with anyone else until one day we saw this seven- or eight-year-old girl hopping over cracks in the sidewalk. And her hair was all ratty and her jacket was frayed, but she was having a good old time leaping over cracks. There was just this sort of feeling between me and my lover, and we grabbed her. We took her to the mall, bought her this Bugs Bunny bomber jacket that she loved and some patent leather shoes she picked out. We took her to Chinese and taught her how to use chopsticks. Then we took her back. This was before the Fendi became popular, but it turned out no one was looking for her anyway. I've no idea what happened to that girl, and to be honest, my lover and I don't really talk about

---

[25] Attempts to contact and interview an actual grabber, of course, were fruitless and in vain. The attachment to anonymity continues a decade and a half later. The author did, in fact, contact many grabbees, but that's it as far as first-hand knowledge goes. The source information remains, and probably ever shall, one-sided.

it. Just sort of think of it and smile together,
you know?'

Colin's remarks suggest a happy-go-lucky
conspiracy, a kind of benevolent coup that one
person wouldn't have the guts to do without another
to egg him on. The couples[26] came upon the idea and
it blossomed at the urging of both. This would
explain the 'euphoric' atmosphere so many grabbees
note, feeling the thrill of the danger and rule-
breaking of it all. Unfortunately, given the
anonymity that has remained in place for the last 15
plus years, all of this tantalizing speculation will
have to remain just that.

'A Sweepstakes Appeal'

'I remember there was this air of excitement
hanging around the neighborhood and especially
the school. We'd all seen groomgrabbing talked
about on TV and the web, and everyone was coming
up with reasons why it would or wouldn't happen
in Monmouth[27]. People were saying it was too

---

[26] And grabbers generally seem to have been couples, that is, lovers who
were in a relationship together. At least, that would seem to be the
impression among the grabbees whose viewpoint, granted, was a bit
young to be judging intimacies among adults.

[27] Small town in northwestern Oregon. Coincidentally, Bopp's school was
one of the seven buildings in Monmouth demolished in 2004 when a
piece of the 'forgotten' Russian space station Horosho hurtled through
the atmosphere, making for a lot of embarrassed apologizing on the
diplomatic front.

small. Other people were saying that's exactly
why someone *would* be grabbed from Monmouth,
because most of the grabs were happening in small
towns. You know, it's like when there's a super
huge Powerball Jackpot, like that one last year
that got up to two billion? Everyone talks about
it, everyone wants it, nobody really thinks
anybody will, but everybody secretly hopes[28].'

Elizabeth Bopp-Twernig,

Grabbed aged seven in 2000

Bopp-Twernig mentions an aspect of groomgrabbing
also discussed by Blandershot-Fields in the UHH
study. She (Blandershot-Fields) writes that as the
trend spread and the months passed, groomgrabbing
began to take on 'a sweepstakes appeal. The
grabbings came, in a surprisingly short amount of
time, to be regarded as a prize, a luck of the draw
windfall which anyone's child could win.' Anyone
else's child, that is. According to an *Us-People*
sidebar feature at the time, parents tended to
preface any comment about groomgrabbing with
something along the lines of 'Well, *my* child will
never be grabbed because he/she has so many friends
and is so well-loved, I can't ever imagine him/her
looking quite pathetic or lonely enough to be
grabbed. For everyone else, however . . .'

This was, of course, more or less an outright lie

---

[28] An impressively apt description of the lottery, which is hardly surprising
as Bopp-Twernig's series of editorials on consensual crime law was
shortlisted for this year's Pulitzer.

on the part of the parents. Economics Nobel Laureate
Ken Kern-Terwilliger of the AT&T Gallup Nielsen
Institute calls this phenomenon the 'Martin Cramwell
Would Be a Terrible Governor; Long Live Governor
Cramwell' Effect[29] in which poll participants, afraid
of the opinion of the polltaker, lie about their
real feelings. As a matter of fact, parents were
actively placing their children in solitary spots:
leaving them with only a ratty tennis ball at the
public park, say, or forcing them to walk any number
of miles home from school. National statistics of
child neglect cases covering the years before,
during, and after the height of the trend look like
an especially precipitious bell curve[30].

---

[29] After the millennial Governor of the State of Washington who trailed his
more moderate and, it turned out, far saner opponent by upwards of
forty-seven per cent in polls going into the election, an election which
he then won by 17,000 votes. It turned out voters were far too embar-
rassed to admit to pollsters that they supported the, ahem, colorful
Cramwell. After the ensuing conflagration, loss of life, *in absentia*
impeachment hearings, mass suicide, and consequent move of the
state's capital from Olympia to Everett in Cramwell's second year, it was
nearly impossible to find anyone who would ever have admitted voting
for him in the first place, although you can't really blame them. The
effect is also blamed for the fall of France to Greenpeace in 2009, as
well as Finland's hostile takeover of Norway in 2013 and, to a smaller
extent, the election of U.S. President D. Rumsfeld and Vice President P.
Anderson Lee in 2008.

[30] Neglectful or groomgrab-hopeful parents were often turned in by an
older generation of grandparents who just about had to glue their
mouths shut to get their jaws off the floor. The author's own grandfather
has a decade-old rant spouting incredulity on the actions of parents
during the groomgrab period, most especially the author's own. The
rant remains the same, as does the degree of passion accompanying it.
The family has learned to not bring the subject up.

Not that it mattered. Colin, in the interview
quoted earlier, indicates that groomgrabbers were
expert at picking out fakes:

> Are you kidding? We have to spend all our
> lives secretly looking for other gay people in
> things like church and work and school. Oblivious
> is one thing we're *not*.

Most fakes were easy to spot. As Colin puts it,
'Children in stained white t-shirts do not bounce
rubber balls off blacktop wearing Kenneth Cole
shoes.' Even more easily, all groomgrabbers usually
had to do was ask if there was any doubt.
Paradoxically, a child instructed to look like an
appealing candidate to a groomgrabber would usually
want to please the grabber so much that they would
reveal the lie in an effort to win trust. Children
don't really learn irony until they get to Joseph
Heller in the eighth grade.

As it is, every major study has attempted to
cross-section the 'average' groomgrabbee and has come
up lacking. Both the UMNHVIPBSL study and especially
Blandershot-Fields cross-referenced, graphed, mapped,
collated, coded, signified, indexed, concordanced,
cataloged, enumerated, scheduled, classified, and
alphabetized the grabbees until finally throwing up
their hands in frustration. The youngest grabbee was
four, the oldest thirteen, and about all anyone has
been able to generalize is that groomgrabbees were
between four and thirteen.

Grabbees were evenly split between boys and
girls. They fell along racial lines at roughly the
same rate as represented in the population. There
were grabbings in all fifty-two current states plus
Guam, with the only even mild statistical spike
being a larger-than-average number of grabbings in
Alaska[31]. Interestingly enough, the grabs cut across
all financial and social strata as well, which would
seem to contradict the point of the groomgrab.
Booher, the first grabee, makes for an interesting
study on this matter. West LA at the time was a
fairly wealthy neighborhood. Booher, who it turned
out lived in a $2 million home and had a six-figure
trust fund, should not necessarily have been a test
case for looking like poverty. Nonetheless, despite
his wealth, as his groomgrabber Roddick said, 'Money
doesn't always mean a kid's not going to fall
through the cracks.' To which Marshall added, 'Or
have appropriate taste.' The grabbers seemed to
concentrate on how pathetic the grabbee seemed
rather than his or her financial background. Another
reason for the demographic well-roundedness of the
grabbees might be the much-discussed notion of
homosexuality as a vertical minority, encapsulating
bits from every other group including the rich and
the poor. As Blandershot-Fields writes, 'Maybe it's
as simple as they went with what they knew.'

---

[31] As Blandershot-Fields notes in one of her less academic moments,
'What *else* do they have to do up there?'

Official Reactions: A Note To Historians

Of course, groomgrabbing was, by any definition, as
illegal as treason, and future historians removed
from the *zeitgeist* might quite credibly wonder where
the hell the authorities were in all this? But
picture if you will the state of the country at the
time: The manned Mars mission had been sabotaged by
extremist MarsFirst!ers; the Namibian Potato-Chip
Debacle had its claws deep into the nation's
economy, sending unemployment into double digits;
and the Argentinian War victory was turning out,
thanks to the MSCNN investigation, to be even more
Pyrrhic than previously thought. Malaise wasn't even
the word for it; the country was downright morose[32].
It's the same reason Bonnie and Clyde and the James
Brothers became cultural heroes at earlier parts of
the previous century.

The Winfrey Administration, naturally, reacted to
the trend with what became its legendary pragmatism.
On February 17, 2001, shortly after the inauguration,
the White House issued a press release stating, 'I
don't see anyone getting hurt. In fact, I see people
getting helped. What's the problem?' Not a single
one of the over four-thousand known incidents of

---

[32] Things got to be so circular and reflexive that the most common movie
bad guys went from being splinter-group Muslim terrorists to actual
movie studios and executives: q.v. *Rush Hour: Product Placement*, *No
Matter How Hard I Try I Still Can't Quite Shake What You Did Eight
Summers Ago* (a movie so ironic and self-reflexive both the heroes *and*
the anti-heroes commit suicide), and Tarantino's unwatchable, five-hour
Fuck the Producers, Man! They Fucking Suck!

groomgrabbing resulted in even an arrest[33]. Local
politicians typically opposed it until they met
someone who was groomgrabbed, then the issue just
dropped[34]. The official opinion seemed to be a need
to condemn groomgrabbing, but secretly, everyone
liked it and wanted it to go on.

At the bottom of it all, like so many other
things about groomgrabbing, the true cause for the
lack of reaction remains elusive.

The End

As does, it seems, the end of groomgrabbing. The
last known groomgrabbing was on November 3, 2002[35],
and after that, nothing. There weren't even
scattered grabs or copycat grabs. What happened? Why
did it stop? It's a circular question that leads
back to why it began in the first place. A whim
meets opportunity, and then the whim leaves.
Blandershot-Fields touches on the subject only

---

[33] Including Booher's parents mentioned at the top of this report. Within a
month, they had dropped the charges and signed a book deal.

[34] There weren't even many conspiracy theories. Televangelist Rob
Patrickson tried many times to raise the issue of a 'left-wing, homosex-
ually agendad [*sic*]' plot to 'ruin our precious children.' But in order to
get the details on the conspiracy, you had to mail the Patrickson
ministries two hundred dollars, your social security number, and a hand-
writing sample, so that never really went anywhere.

[35] Jackson Hurd, aged nine, from Scottsboro, Alabama. His grabbers (a
pair, as always) dressed him in new Levi's and new boots, then took
him to a funny-car race. Hurd is now a Republican ('though very
moderate') U.S. Representative from Alabama's Fourth Congressional
District.

briefly[36], but suggests that groomgrabbing simply ran its course the way all trends do.

The author has another theory. Rather more than a theory, actually. An unknown fact of groomgrabbing, not shared with any of the studies so far discussed in any forum, is the fact that all groomgrabbers imparted a single instruction to all grabbees. The author knows this because, as previously stated, he was a groomgrabbee himself. He has confirmed this with numerous private interviews with other groomgrabbees[37] who are in agreement that the time for the instruction is near. They have graciously agreed to let the author be the first to make the instruction known, partially because this format[38] lends itself so nicely to rumor.

The instructions were simply, 'Pass it on.'

The way all trends do, groomgrabbing is going to make a comeback.

The first groomgrabbing of the second wave happens sometime next month[39].

---

[36] Her main focus being profiles of the grabbees.

[37] Who would only discuss the secret with a fellow grabbee. The author will not name them because part of the instruction is to pretend that there were no instructions. Any grabbees mentioned by name in this paper will profess no knowledge of these instructions.

[38] I.e. an unsourced, undergraduate term paper.

[39] If pressed, the author will deny having said any of the things contained within this paper.

Ponce de Leon is a retired
married couple from Toronto

From Elizabeth Bronwyn, Public Health Nurse (Ret.), Toronto, Ontario, to Dr Wayne Bronwyn, Ophthalmologist, Boston, Massachusetts. Handwritten. Mailed from unknown address, presumed to be central Australia.

Son,

As we've said many times, your father and I are enormously grateful to you for this trip. Our fortieth wedding anniversary has turned out to be the best we've ever had (except, perhaps, our always irreplaceable first). Our time here has been so wonderful, and we've come to know such great joy. *Great* Joy. How can I even say it? I can't, son, I just can't, and I don't know if I'll ever be able to communicate it to you in any way that you'll understand until you're older yourself.

We're staying. There's no way around it, so there it is. We're staying. For good.

I know this is a great shock to you. Knowing you, you probably have some strong feelings on the matter, and six weeks ago, we'd have thought we were as crazy as you're thinking right now. But such things have happened here, such wondrous, *remindful* things that have invigorated us. We've suddenly and unexpectedly rediscovered what it means to have new experiences and a new outlook. When you're our age, I hope you'll be lucky enough to know what it's like to have your first completely new point of view in twenty years.

Through a friend of ours back home, we've already arranged the sale of the house. (We've known someone who's wanted it for years; he was only too happy that we finally obliged. Don't worry, we're getting our money's worth.) Because we're from the Commonwealth, immigration doesn't look to be a problem either, especially considering that my health and your father's are excellent. (See what you missed when you naturalized? The only place in the world Americans are welcome to stay is America. And you, especially; a doctor in a country with no nationalized medicine. Tut tut, one last time.)

Yes, I know, what in the blazes are we thinking? After 61 years, what can I say? When you know, you know.

Your father says not to kick yourself for giving us the trip. You've no idea what a wonderful thing you've done.

All our love,
[signed]
Mom & Dad

P.S. We'll write soon.

From Dr Wayne Bronwyn, to Derek Bell, Executive Secretary to Ambassador Margaret Gottscheid, United States Embassy, Canberra, Australia. Via facsimile.

Mr Bell:

Per our phone conversation of today, I am faxing you the letter I received from my parents, Mr Henry L. and Mrs Elizabeth 'Beth' R. Bronwyn, this morning.

As I cannot possibly reiterate too clearly, the letter is so utterly out of keeping with any pattern of observed behavior that I am led to conclude that they are almost certainly being held in Australia against their will through unknown circumstances or by some unknown person.

To summarize what I attempted to express over the phone, here in short are the reasons I am alarmed:

(1) My mother describes her health and the health of my father as 'excellent.' This cannot possibly be the case. My mother is 61 and my father 62. In addition, my father has high blood pressure, and my mother has migraine headaches. It was only after extensive consultation with their physicians that I went ahead with the gift of the trip, a trip that was originally planned at two weeks

and which my parents themselves suspiciously extended to six. And for that matter, why bring the subject of their health up at all?

(2)   I do not care how much anyone wants to sell a house, it seems highly unlikely that the entire transaction can be secured between two parties at entirely different points on the globe in a few weeks' time. As they did not provide the name of the 'friend,' I have been unable to find out any further on the matter as of today, although I did talk to Mrs Olive Ray, a close friend of my mother's. Mrs Ray had not heard of any such deal or of any plan of my parents' to stay in Australia. This leads to reason number three.

(3)   My mother would not have kept such a thing from Mrs Ray. She, Mrs Ray, seemed to think that the matter was not cause for much concern, that my parents had been struck by a fancy which would pass or that perhaps they were merely playing some sort of prank, the source of the prank being their ongoing enjoyment at my expense for becoming a naturalized U.S. citizen after marriage to my wife. My mother even refers to this in her letter, but in such a way as to prompt reason number four.

(4)   My mother says 'Tut tut, one last time.' What exactly can 'one last time' mean? This is ominous evidence indeed.

I have included my parents' itinerary, although they did veer from it since they extended their trip. I have also included a blown-up and darkened copy of the envelope in which the letter was sent in hopes that the postmark might be of some help.

Fax me back as soon as possible with some kind of response. My parents are elderly, and I am greatly concerned that harm has fallen them. In the meantime, I am going to do some work of my own to get to the bottom of this. I am more than prepared to fly to Australia if that is what is required.

As a naturalized citizen, I trust I can expect the same assistance from your Embassy as any native-born American. I'll hear from you soon.

[signed]
Dr Wayne Bronwyn.

From Derek Bell to Dr Wayne Bronwyn. Via facsimile.

Dr Bronwyn:

The Embassy is in receipt of your fax dated 6 October. The fax follows our lengthy phone conversation of the same date. We are still looking into just exactly why you were mysteriously cut off, Dr Bronwyn, and also why you were not able to re-connect to my office. At any rate, on to your fax.

As I attempted to explain to you over the phone before we were cut off, I am not sure what you would like us to do in this matter. You said in our conversation that your parents were of sound mind when they left on the trip, and though it seems plausible that one older person might possibly lose their bearings on an overseas trip, it seems unlikely that *both* would, especially considering that you yourself felt strongly enough to send them on a trip by themselves halfway around the world. Also, while 61 and 62 are somewhat up there in years, I don't know many people who would call that *elderly*. The Ambassador is 66 herself, and hale as ever. If your parents were in their late eighties, for example, I would be more inclined to lean towards some sort of mysterious circumstances or scam, again going on the inference that you believed enough in their mental states and personal health to send them on the trip in the first place.

In addition, I have never heard of any scam coming out of Australia's center dealing with the mysterious actions of older tourists. It's a big, red desert with a few oases, and the tourist trade there is too valuable to have missed any such scam happening on any scale. For that matter, I suddenly find myself unclear on exactly what sort of scam you might be talking about.

It is my personal tendency to read the letter from your parents at face value. Take it from a career diplomat who has been here for 18 years: this is an amazing place. Perhaps what happened is just what your parents say happened. They were rekindled by a change of landscape. It's not unknown. Some retirees move to Florida, looking for Ponce de Leon's Fountain of Youth, no doubt. Your parents have just chosen a different hot climate that's farther away.

This, however, is all moot speculation, because, as you somehow failed to mention in our nearly forty-minute conversation, your parents are citizens of Canada. Although I can understand that you were quite excited and might have easily forgotten such a detail, the fact is, our office has no jurisdiction over them whatsoever. I suggest if you wish to pursue the matter that you contact the Canadian Embassy. I have included their phone and fax numbers.

Might I also suggest that if you do in fact call our good friends to the north, you might receive closer care to your problem if you choose, shall we say, somewhat less frank language than you engaged in during our phone conversation. Your fax strikes quite a nice tone (perhaps Mrs Bronwyn helped?), and this is probably the best route with our Canadian friends. Remember, they're like Americans, only more British.

Yours,
[signed]
Derek Bell

From Elizabeth Bronwyn, to Dr Wayne Bronwyn. Hand-written. Mailed from unknown address, presumed to be central or southeastern Australia.

Son,

I'm sorry for the delay. We had intended to write you immediately with our new address, but so much has gone on in the past few weeks that there's been barely a moment to put pen to paper. A new friend of ours has set up a post office box for us (address enclosed) in Binturang Springs, which is where we've been staying for the past several days. We needed to establish a permanent address for immigration purposes. We hope to have a resident visa sometime soon. As it is, we've decided to spend the remaining time on our tourist visa traveling around this beautiful country.

I was planning on telling you all this in our phone conversation yesterday, but you were so upset, it was difficult to get any words out. Then we were somehow cut off. Must be these international phone lines.

I do understand that you're upset, son. I can certainly understand the shock at your parents suddenly pulling up stakes and moving 11,000 miles but, once again, what can I say? We've found a new outlook, a new life. As vague as that is, it's the best way I can put it. Not all older people, not *most*, want simply to wind their days down in a sameness that lasts until you stop breathing.

Why die before you die? Your father and I have done something daring for probably the first time since we got married. Out of character? Sure. But isn't acting out of character part of character, too? I hope we can talk again soon, and I can try to convince you one more time that sometimes these things just happen.

One more thing, I hardly think that moving away when you're 39 years old constitutes 'abandonment.' You have Jane and the kids. We only ever visited once or twice a year; hardly lifeblood to either of us, if we're honest. I'll chalk up most of your remarks to shock at our decision. Hopefully soon you'll come to understand.

As I've said, we're very, very busy, so I'll end here. I think it's clear, given the phone trouble, that letters are a better means of communication for us. All of our mail will be forwarded from the P.O. Box, so feel free to write at any time. We'll get the letter and respond from whatever port of call we've set our feet onto.

Love to everyone,
[signed]
Mom & Dad

From Dr Wayne Bronwyn to Philip Wilder, KBE, Ambassador, Commonwealth of Canada, Canberra, Australia. Via Facsimile.

Mr Ambassador Wilder,

As I have received next to no help from your 'assistant,' I am writing to you directly and demanding your help. My parents, Canadian citizens, have fallen prey to mysterious circumstances and are either being held in Australia against their will or are mentally incapable of making the proper decision to return home. I have included two letters from my mother as proof that something is amiss. I have also included my correspondence with the American Embassy in Canberra, who were of no help whatsoever. I trust you'll make it a matter of national pride to do better.

To be frank, my parents have always been stilted people of limited imagination. I know that sounds cruel coming from a son, but I mean it lovingly. They have lived in the same house in Toronto for my entire life. My father was an accountant for 40 years, my mother a nurse for 38. They are just not given to flights of fancy, certainly nothing as ridiculous as selling everything they own on the spur of the moment and moving halfway around the world. These are people of limited horizons! For the past five decades, their idea of a good time has been a drive to the same lake once a season! It took months of convincing for them to even take this one vacation, and I nearly had to force them onto the plane myself. I only persisted because of what my wife calls my 'dogheaded dedication to the impossible task,' a stubbornness you would do well to keep in mind.

Additionally, I spoke to my mother on the phone a few days ago for the first time since they reached this 'decision.' Her answers to my questions were vague and directionless. She kept saying 'these things just happen' and 'I can't explain it.' Even when I pressed, she was unable to give me a straight answer.

This is clearly a cry for help. Something is wrong. Something is so obviously wrong that I cannot believe the cavalier attitude taken by some of those on your staff. And this plus the fact that I was disconnected four times in a row. I am providing you with the post office box that my mother gave for her address, and I want someone to look into it. I was a Canadian citizen until I married my lovely wife thirteen years ago. I can only hope that my expatriate country can give me assistance that can only be considered just and decent.

I want some answers. As I have said, if I get none, I will come to that godforsaken country myself.

Yours,
[signed]
Dr Wayne Bronwyn

From Ambassador Philip Wilder, KBE, to Dr Wayne Bronwyn. Via Facsimile.

My dear Dr Bronwyn,

You've developed quite a reputation in our office for your persistence. I am not sure whether it is Canadian pugnaciousness reborn or a healthily adapted American tenacity, but you most certainly have gotten our attention, which, I trust, was your whole point.

I have reviewed all your correspondence, as well as the notes my talented deputy, Anita, compiled on your telephone calls. I wonder, as a sidenote, whether you have perhaps misread as 'cavalier' nothing more than the relaxed attitude folks tend to adopt in a tropical clime. Remember, it is deep, glorious spring here, where our outlooks, while hopefully remaining professional, have nonetheless gained a rosy tint. Don't judge us harshly, Dr Bronwyn, the sun here would cause your president himself to not only remove his shirt, but to not feel embarrassed about it.

I must say that my first inclination is to agree with my esteemed associate in the American office. While the behaviour of your parents may be accurately labeled extraordinary, I would say it is delightfully rather than ominously so. I am 63 years of age myself, and although I will miss dearly the people and trees of my beloved Vancouver, I'm staying in this wonderful place when I

57

retire this autumn. And me, a knighted civil servant, no less, giving up my home country for one that will probably discharge the monarchy any moment now.

But I digress. Because of your persuasive, albeit somewhat quixotic tactics, I have had my office look into the matter of your parents as much as is legally and ethically possible. Your parents have broken no laws, remember, and not everyone sees the obvious foul play that you do. Nevertheless, your commitment to your belief is stirring enough for us to have uncovered the following:

1. Your mother and father requested immigration proceedings on September 21, some weeks before your mother's first letter. Perhaps given your reaction to the news, she was deliberating on ways to soften the blow, as it were.

2. A post office box was indeed established in Binturang Springs. We have been in contact with the clerk who rented the box. He remembers the box being rented by a young woman. He says that she was friendly and otherwise unremarkable except that her voice seemed slightly accented, meaning of course, slightly accented *Australian*. This would seem to be the 'new friend' that your mother refers to in her second letter. As you can see, despite your accusations, your letters were indeed read. Let me also, as a sidenote, just say that Binturang Springs is a very small town, as are most in central Australia. Tourists have a very high visibility, making the likelihood of foul play even

more remote as any larcenous behaviour could not possibly be kept hidden for long. It's a big place, the red centre, but an empty one. You can see from one horizon to the other and everything in-between. Only the aborigines know the secrets, and they're not telling.

3. Though we have checked some cursory leads tracking older travelers from Binturang, this office has been unable to locate your parents. Apart from simply sending a letter and asking them, finding out where your parents' mail is being forwarded is illegal unless we have clear just cause, and I am sorry, Dr Bronwyn, I don't see just cause anywhere in this situation.

Perhaps you should just believe what your parents have told you and be happy for them in their newfound youth, if you will. And frankly, even if you will not, it is my duty to inform you that this office will aid you no further. Again, I can understand your passion and even forgive the rough edges with which you pursue it, but I can see no reason for my office or the government of Canada to put more resources into what is bordering on harassment of two adults acting legally.

You are welcome to follow through on your wish to write the Canadian Foreign Affairs Ministry concerning our actions in this matter. I am confident we will be easily acquitted.

Having said all this, if more, or rather *any* hard evidence comes to light or if you are not satisfied with ending your investigation here, which I strongly suspect is the case, you may want to contact the Australian Ministry of Immigration here in Canberra. They would certainly be interested if there were any hint of immigration fraud. There is clearly not; I am only suggesting a tactic you might use, again, if you insist on pursuing the matter. I make the suggestion because I believe in your sincerity, despite your casually deleterious way with spoken language.

If you decide to come to this country as part of your quest, might I suggest that you not miss the opportunity to visit any one of the larger cities' Royal Botanical Gardens? The bulk of tourist highlights are well-covered in most guidebooks, but I find that visitors often overlook the abundant gardens available here. Most are lovely for a leisurely stroll, like those I used to take in Stanley Park, only not so often gray.

I will leave you here, Dr Bronwyn. Good luck in your future endeavours, and please refrain from contacting this office in the future.

Your humble servant,
[signed]
Ambassador Philip Wilder, KBE

From Elizabeth Bronwyn, to Mrs Olive Ray, Public Health Nurse (Ret.), Toronto, Ontario, Canada. Handwritten. International Express Mail from the Cavalcade Hotel, Perth, Australia.

Ollie,

Here are the tickets and the cashier's check. Henry and I can't wait to see you. We can't wait for you to see *us*. You won't believe the change, and I mean that in ways you can't possibly imagine. You won't regret coming, and I have very little doubt we can persuade you to make the same decision we did. It's unbelievable here, Ollie, in all the best ways.

Your plane leaves on the 3rd and, because of the way the dateline works, arrives here on the 5th. We've become close to a young couple with whom we have a lot in common (you'll see what I mean; Henry says, 'Boy, will you ever!'). They're going to pick you up at the airport. Don't worry, we'll see each other shortly afterward. You can write to Paul after you get here and explain everything. Trusting me on this issue is essential.

Swallow your trepidation and brush away your fears. If there was any time in your life to act in the face of caution, it's now. You've earned it after all these years of living. We both know you're only old when you decide to be. Decide not to be, Ollie.

Looking forward to seeing you,
[signed]
Liz

From Elizabeth Bronwyn, to Dr Wayne Bronwyn. Hand-written. Mailed from unknown address, presumed to be central Australia.

Son,

There is going to come a day when I'm finally going to be fed up with you. I thought today might be that day. I'm referring, of course, to the outlandish, embarrassing, and ultimately infuriating phone call I have just been put through with the gentleman from the Australian Ministry of Immigration.

Do not think, as has been your tendency for far too long for me to expect you to act any differently, that it was anything but *you* that got me angry. The gentleman was quite polite and friendly, even charming, as he went through his list of humiliating questions about supposed actions of ours that you've insinuated. Questions about our sanity, our health, our finances.

Then, my dearest son, questions about our alleged criminal pasts, our financial dire straits in previous years, *our possible willingness to smuggle drugs*. You couldn't have implied diamonds or rare birds, could you? Obviously you thought it would direct them to us most quickly (and it did), but I would have thought that even in your haste you might have realized that the idea of two sixty-something drug smugglers, from *Canada* no less, is nothing short of absurd.

How dare you, you child? How dare you slander us so grotesquely because you are simply too selfish to see that we've acted of our own free will? Being unable to abide our decision is one thing, but what you've done is nothing short of dangerous. I'm trying my hardest to view this as some misguided idea of loving behavior on your part, but I am having difficulty.

Almost the only thing that keeps me from cutting you off completely is that the good people at the Ministry of Immigration clearly believe you're as loony as we think you are. I doubt most suspected drug smugglers get off with a simple phone interview. Can you imagine in the midst of your frenzy how awful such an accusation could have been for us? I'm sure you think everything would have turned out okay, but what if it hadn't? What if things had gone horribly wrong? What if they weren't so inclined to listen? What if your father and I had had to sit in jail while we waited for you to come and clear things up? Is any of this getting through to you?

And all this as we're suffering the death of Olive Ray, which, in your investigative zeal, you must have discovered and, it must be concluded, disregarded its impact on your father and me. We were unable to return for the funeral, so if you showed up and looked for us there, I hope you at least had the good grace to leave some flowers.

How dare you? That's my benediction, son. Consider it clearly. How dare you?
[signed]
Mother.

From Dr Wayne Bronwyn to Brian Coppedge, Senior Investigator, Australian Ministry of Immigration, Canberra, Australia. Handwritten. Mailed from Hughes Gaol, Darwin, Australia.

Mr Coppedge:

I am writing this letter to you because of the increasing difficulties I have had in getting through to your office by phone, a problem exacerbated by the limited phone privileges I have in here. I find it hard to believe, in a modern Western country like Australia, my phone calls would be cut off so often, even when I'm calling from this little bunch of shacks you people have chosen to name after Darwin.

In a final attempt in what I see as my increasingly futile search for my parents, I will recap the events that led me here to try and get someone, *anyone*, in this godforsaken ~~shithole~~ desert of a country to help me track them down.

As you know (as I have explained to your belligerent staff many, *many* times), a week after the last letter I received from my mother (enclosed), I received a phone call from Paul Ray, son of Olive Ray, a close friend of my mother. As indicated in my mother's letter, Mrs Ray suffered a massive stroke and died shortly after this whole farrago began. Because of funeral arrangements and family responsibilities, Paul Ray was unable to go

65

through his mother's effects in any detailed fashion for several weeks, but when he did he discovered a letter from my mother urging Mrs Ray to fly to Perth (enclosed) along with plane tickets and a check for expenses.

Paul Ray then contacted me. He indicated that he had spoken to my mother the day after the funeral, when she called to speak with Mrs Ray. He told her the news of Mrs Ray's death and said that my mother took it badly. He was surprised that my mother didn't already know, as he remembered the two women being friends, but, having had somewhat limited contact with his mother for several years, he thought nothing further of it until he found the letter and plane tickets. He told me that my mother made no mention of inviting Olive to Australia and *did not even mention that she was calling from there.* How many more odd circumstances do I need to point out before someone will take me seriously?

I then contacted your office again (even after you had done such a botched job of investigating their activities. A *phone* interview for possible drug smugglers? What's *wrong* with you people?) and offered this new information. I was rebuked and, indeed, told to stop 'harassing' my own parents. Harassing? I'm trying to get to the bottom of a very serious situation. Why can't anyone see that I am motivated by nothing but compassion and concern?

Receiving no assistance whatsoever from your office (or in fact anyone at all throughout this whole ordeal; I've already sent you copies of the letters from the American and Canadian Embassies that show just how outrageously I've been handled), I took a trip to this blackened landscape myself, and in the past six weeks, I have been to every bare corner of it.

I first went to Binturang Springs, the location of the post office box, and talked to a Mr George Kingfisher, manager of the inn where my parents initially stayed. After trying with limited success to convince him of the desperation of the situation, he finally directed me to Henry Badgery, a tour operator who had conducted my parents on a personalized tour of the surrounding desert area. Mr Badgery said that he remembered my parents, that they were pleasant people, that they had befriended a young married couple, but he told me nothing more. I did not and do not trust this Mr Badgery, let me tell you right now. I am almost certain he's a liar.

I then contacted the Binturang Springs Post Office, where I was thwarted in my attempt to discover my parents' current forwarding address by a callous postal clerk named Armando Bravada who refused to bend the rules despite the obvious gravity of the situation.

Having received no help, I embarked upon what ended up being a nearly complete circle of your country. I flew to Perth, where my parents had earlier planned to meet Olive Ray if she had been able to use the tickets they sent. I visited the hotel indicated on the return address of the Express Mail to Mrs Ray, but no one gave me any useful information. I then headed east along your southern coast, following backwards the middle part of my parents' original itinerary through impossibly named towns like Wagga Wagga and Wollongong. I took a dip down to Hobart, then back up to Melbourne, through Canberra (where your office was closed due to some royal holiday or other), then to Sydney and up to Brisbane and Cairns. Occasionally, I came across people who thought they recognized my parents' names but not the pictures I provided. On the whole, I found out very little.

It finally occurred to me while driving the considerable miles between resorts scattered along your northeast coastline that my method had been a thoroughly inefficient way to canvass for my parents. Actual Australia was much bigger than the picture I contained in my mind. It seems obvious, but I have been recently upset and my concern has sometimes taken over the better part of my reason. I realized there were a lot more people here than I'd thought, and I couldn't just go looking without some guidelines. Again, embarrassingly obvious, but once you get an idea in your head, it's hard to shake it.

It was at this point that I returned to Binturang Springs and, unable to find either Mr Kingfisher or Mr Badgery, I paid another visit to Mr Bravada.

Having had some long hours in my cell to reflect, I can honestly say that I regret that I acted like less than a gentleman to Mr Bravada. Although I would hardly regard my contact with him as 'assault' or 'false imprisonment,' it would seem that the Western Australia authorities disagreed enough to contact their Darwin counterparts. If I ever see Mr Bravada again, I would do my best to apologize. My arrest, though extremely inconvenient, is beside the point, however.

I was able to get two interesting bits of information

out of Mr Bravada. One was my parents' current forwarding address here in Darwin (enclosed). The second was a telling comment about this Mr Badgery. Mr Bravada didn't know all that much about Mr Badgery (or was keeping it to himself) but was able, after exhaustive interrogation, to tell me, and I quote, 'Some people say that he [Mr Badgery] takes old folks out into the bush and brings young folks back.'

Due to an unexpected loss of consciousness, Mr Bravada was unable to tell me anything more, but my concern for my parents' wellbeing immediately increased. Using the address Mr Bravada had provided, I flew to Darwin and went straight to my parents' hotel. The front desk clerk told me that there were a Mr and Mrs Bronwyn checked in. The young woman had not checked them in herself, but a bellhop thought he remembered a young couple by that name. Undoubtedly, these are the 'friends' my mother mentions in her letters. He believed that they had mentioned an older couple travelling with them and perhaps (there was some confusion) he had misheard who, in fact, was named Bronwyn.

You can imagine my dismay that it was at this moment, when I finally had some answers within reach, that I was accosted by the Darwin Police and taken away.

So, here I sit in Hughes Jail (or Gaol, is it?), awaiting heaven knows what fate, and I'm asking one last time for your help, Mr Coppedge.

I've been thinking through scenarios that might have engulfed my parents, and I think I've figured it out. It involves Mr Badgery, and I shudder to think of it. He 'takes old folks out and brings young folks back in.' It's clearly some sort of immigration scam. Mr Badgery lures some older folks into a tour group, takes them out to a desolate area, does dire misdeeds to them, and replaces them with younger couples who want to immigrate who then assume the identities of the 'older folks.' I am sure Mr Badgery makes a tidy profit.

Murder is what I'm talking about, Mr Coppedge, something much more serious than these trumped-up 'assault' charges for which I sit imprisoned. I contend that my parents have been murdered by Mr Badgery and their identities have been assumed by a younger couple who have written letters as my mother saying that they've 'suddenly decided to stay.' It's the only explanation that fits.

Unless, of course, Mr Badgery has actually found a fountain of youth, but even I am not yet desperate enough to believe that.

It's so clear, Mr Coppedge, *so clear* what's happened. I apologize for any past rash behavior on my part in my eagerness to find the truth, but there is murder most foul here and I humble myself and beg you one last time to investigate.

Very truly yours,
[signed]
Dr Wayne Bronwyn

Letter from Brian Coppedge, Australian Ministry of Immigration, to Dr Wayne Bronwyn, Darwin Jail. Hand delivered by messenger.

Dr Bronwyn:

Let me begin by saying that you have become the stuff of legend here at the Immigration Ministry, right alongside the Filipino man who had a sex-change operation so he could marry his Australian friend and become a citizen (made even stranger by the fact that the gentleman knew that we allow homosexual partners to immigrate yet went ahead with the operation anyway) and the Romanian woman who was not satisfied with just one Australian husband and somehow managed to wed four. You're going into our folklore as the Son Who Harangued His Parents Right Out of Their Own Country.

You may well find this insulting, but, after your verbal tirades, threats, and extraordinary actions, I feel little compunction to hide my personal distaste for you. You should, however, take it as a measure of pride. Even after you've left this country for good, which, I assure you, will be sooner rather than later, you'll be remembered.

All rancor aside (or most anyway), your behaviour has been of such astonishing effort that, as a parting gift, we have investigated enough of your claims to file this matter away permanently.

Although we have yet to schedule an in-person interview (one step among many in the long immigration process: immigration doesn't just *happen*, you know – we *do* look into things), I have spoken to your mother several times by telephone. She has been helpful in providing both factual details of their vacation as well as illuminating anecdotes about her son's particular person-ality quirks. I can safely say that there is no doubt in my mind that your parents are safe and sound and simply wish to immigrate to this great country. I have also spoken with Mr Kingfisher, general manager of the Hollingsworth Hotel in Binturang Springs, as well as Messrs Badgery and Bravada, who, at the behest of our office, has generously agreed to not press charges in exchange for your prompt expulsion from the country.

First of all, Dr Bronwyn, your murder claim is little short of ridiculous. As I've said, I have spoken many times to your mother by phone myself, and though she is somewhat confused and embarrassed by your persistence, she is vibrant, energetic, and very much alive. She provided details on the sale of their house back in Toronto, details which we independently verified with Canadian authorities, details which no 'immigrant imposter' could possibly know. In addition, we were able to obtain credit card receipts (matched again with cooperation from your mother) from various hotels along their entire itinerary, and signatures from the earlier part of your parents' trip match exactly with signatures from later. If your parents had, in fact, been replaced in some bizarre immigration scam, I would have thought you would have noticed a change in the handwriting of your mother's letters. No one is an exact enough forger to fool a son.

As for Mr Badgery, we have discovered that he is a quite well-liked fixture in Binturang Springs, having led tours as far back as anyone can remember, something along the lines of forty years or more. I highly doubt that he could keep any murderous scheme afloat for four-plus decades and not raise an eyebrow until now. As for Mr Bravada, he recalls saying nothing along the lines of 'old folks going in and young folks coming out,' but then again, he remembers rather little of your attack, so traumatized was he at the literal and figurative brow-beating he underwent at your hands. Once again, you may count yourself very lucky that Mr Bravada has agreed to let you move back to America rather than press charges. You may also count yourself lucky that our office chose to make the case to Mr Bravada to do so. There was strong sentiment here to let you sit in Hughes Gaol for as long as they would have you. However, we are a compassionate country, and as your mental capacities are clearly under some strain, we will choose to believe that you are acting outside your normal operating behaviour.

And that, Dr Bronwyn, is that. We shall do no further investigating, though some of us here believed that we should have ceased after the illegal drug wild goose chase you tried to send us on. The case is closed. We are more than happy to welcome your parents into the country, and we are just as happy to usher you out. Accompanying this letter is an order to escort you to the airport and onto a plane back to America. Do not attempt to enter Australia again, Dr Bronwyn. It would be unwise.

As a last note, may I implore you to get some help once you arrive home? As you are a physician yourself, I hope that you will be able to somehow objectively see your current state of mind and the actions that have resulted. Take our decision not to press charges as a second chance to get some professional assistance for what has clearly been a shock to your psyche. You might start with fear of abandonment issues.

I am confident that you will reject these entreaties out of hand, but despite what you might think, we *are* concerned about your wellbeing. Honestly.

Have a nice flight out. Any further inquiries from yourself or parties representing yourself will be returned unopened.

Good day,
[signed]
Brian Coppedge
Ministry of Immigration

From Jessica Petty, Manager, Terra Australis Hotel, Brisbane, Australia, to Brian Coppedge. Typed. Mailed.

Dear Mr Coppedge,

I must apologize for the delay in my response to your request re: Henry and Elizabeth Bronwyn. We've been in the thick of the summer season, and your request got waylaid. As you haven't contacted us for follow-up since originally calling, I trust that the information you needed wasn't urgent.

As a matter of fact, I remember the Bronwyns clearly. Young Canadian couple, yes? They were here just before Christmas. Exact dates: 21–23 December. I was on desk duty the night of the 22nd. I remember because we had a near-tragedy in our restaurant. A young boy eating at one of the tables began choking. Apparently, Elizabeth Bronwyn was sitting nearby and responded with the Heimlich Manoeuvre. Mrs Bronwyn and her husband were very modest about her actions and declined the family's offer to pay for their hotel stay. I was so struck by the sheer self-effacement with which Mrs Bronwyn treated the whole situation that I made their visit free anyway, which is why I have to report that I don't have the credit card receipts you requested.

At any rate, I have nothing out of the ordinary to report about them, except for the above act of heroism.

They checked out the day after with the best wishes of all our staff.

Once again, I'm sorry for the delay in my response, but hopefully the matter was of as little urgency as your message indicated. These were smart kids, very impressive. I trust they're not in any trouble.

Yours truly,
[signed]
Jessica Petty
Terra Australis Hotel

From Elizabeth Bronwyn, to Dr Wayne Bronwyn. Handwritten. Mailed from unknown address, presumed to be northeastern Australia.

Son,

Your father and I had hoped there would somehow be a way for you to understand our decision to stay here. We had hoped that some day you would be in a frame of mind to be able to clearly comprehend our reasons. It has become obvious that such a day will never arrive.

And more's the shame, too. If you could, at all, appreciate the air and the light here, you might be able to see. The nice man from the Immigration Ministry told us about your sojourn across this great country. I hope you somehow, some way got a taste of this country's rejuvenating powers.

And then you went and got yourself arrested. Arrested! What were you *thinking*? How dangerous were you trying to make yourself? I can only imagine what you might have done if you'd found your father and me. How dare you put us in a position to be afraid of you?

You want to share our lives, but sharing means that we give freely, not that you take. I'm so angry, I can barely see straight. If you only knew what you were missing out on, if there were only some way to get through that thick skull of yours.

There are answers to everything, son, and you've managed to cheat yourself out of all of them. One day, perhaps, cooler heads might prevail, but for now, all I will say is that we've vanished to a new life.

The letter is unsigned.

Jesus' elbows and other
Christian urban myths

Jesus Was Double-Jointed

'They say if you look closely at paintings of Jesus on the cross from the Middle Ages, you can see his arms are bent slightly out. They've done studies, and it turns out that it's because he was actually double-jointed.

'Under normal circumstances, crucifixion killed fairly quickly. After an hour or so, you pretty much suffocated or your heart gave out. They've done studies on this as well.

'Jesus had to stay alive a bit longer because he had his destiny to fulfil, of course. He had to live until he'd converted the two thieves crucified on either side of him and until the sky turned red on Good Friday. But he also had to be all human at the time, too, because that was kind of the whole point. What God did was make him double-jointed, so he was a bit more flexible and could hang there a bit longer, hold himself up, suffer a bit more and live long enough to fulfil his sacrifice. If you look closely at the paintings that hang in Rome, you can see that his elbows bend against the angle slightly more than is normal. It's true, just look. They say it's because of a scripture from Song of Solomon about how "his joints are like jewels".

'Later paintings don't show this, but they say it's because they were painted further away from the actual event.'

The Missing Day

'Like, okay, this guy I know, he has this friend whose uncle works at NASA, right? And so one day, they were, like, routinely checking the positions of the sun, the moon, and the rest of the planets in the solar system, both 100 years ago and projecting up to 100 years from now. They do this to make sure they're mapping all the planets and stuff correctly, because they have to plan the trajectories of, like, satellites and space shuttles and other space craft to make sure nothing runs into anything else, you know? So they won't, like, collide.

'Anyway, it's standard procedure. But so they're doing this checking, and one of the guys, this scientist guy, notices that they're missing, like, a day. Like, a whole day, right? Like, it doesn't make sense, right? So they run it all over again, and then they expand their search even farther backwards and forwards because something's off. They figure, these scientists, they figure somebody either, you know, fed the wrong information into the computers or somebody screwed up comparing the results or *something*, you know? Something went wrong somewhere.

'So they, like, keep doing it, and keep checking everything for accuracy and no one can figure out what's wrong. This day, this one day, just keeps, like, not being there. This one missing day.

'And then this one scientist, who happens to be a Christian, praise God, says he might know what's up, that he might have the answer, right? But that, like, the other scientists might not like what the answer is, okay? Because, you know, it's, like, from *God*, you know? See what I'm saying?

'So these other scientists, they're like, "Well, we don't know any other way, you know, so, like, what have you got?"

'And so like this Christian scientist, well, not a *Christian Scientist*, like, but a scientist who's Christian, yeah? None of that funny business. This scientist goes that he remembers from his Bible readings about a story in Joshua when Joshua's trying to, like, rescue Gideon. And he doesn't have enough time, right? To make the rescue? So he asks God if He'll make the sun stand still, right? Right? See where I'm going? So this scientist thinks this might be the day.

'So the other scientists all go back in their calculations and observations and whatever and find that, in Joshua's time that there's this *missing day*, right? Can you believe it? So they're all, like, scratching their heads and making their observations and wondering just what the heck to make of it because they're *scientists*, right? And this is something out of the *Bible*, okay? But right then, one of the scientists, not the Christian one, obviously, goes, "A-ha! According to these calculations, the time missing here is only 23 hours and 20 minutes. *Not* a whole day. The Bible can't be right."

'So the scientist who's a Christian goes, you know, "Fair enough" but he, like, gets out his Bible, 'cause he keeps it in his desk, and he has a look. And the Bible doesn't say a whole day, it says *about a whole day*, right? Right? And so, he thinks again to his Bible readings and remembers Hezekiah, okay? And he remembers – and he looks it up, too, to show the other scientists – he remembers that Hezekiah was on, like, his death bed. And the prophet Isaiah visits him because God said that Isaiah was going to heal him, right? Hezekiah, you know, though, doesn't, like, *believe* this, because he's dying, right? And so he goes to God, he goes, "Show me, like, a *sign*." You know? "Something to prove that I'll be healed."

'Okay, so God, you know, being God, goes "Okay, I'll give you, like, a choice." He goes, "I'll send the sun forwards or backwards ten degrees." So Hezekiah goes, "Send it backwards, God, and I'll, like, believe in you." So God does, of course. He sends the sun back ten degrees.

'Well, guess what? Ten degrees equals 40 minutes. Right? So 40 minutes plus 23 hours and 20 minutes equals the missing day. They found the missing day. In the Bible.

'One hundred per cent true, I swear.'

President Woodrow Wilson Tried to Be the Antichrist (and Failed)

'Now, let me tell you a little story, very in-te-res-tin. It was in an article in a magazine I read somewhere, I don't remember exackly, but it was about how – and not many people know this – President Woodrow Wilson tried to be the Antichrist. True. There's proof of this, *akchull* proof which scholars have tried to suppress for decades, but it's true. It was uncovered by researchers at the Library of Congress. Woodrow Wilson was a secret member of the Church of Satan. What's more, he was a *high priest* in the Church of Satan and knew *exackly* what he was doing. You can just imagine him sitting there, having used his evil ways to become President, and thinking, "Well, how can I get more power? How can I – what's the word? – *consolidate* my presidency?"

'Like Lucifer himself, he knew his Bible verses, and so he prayed to the Devil, saying "Oh, Dark Lord, how can I become more parrful in your service?" And the Devil answered him, directing him to the Book of the Revelations of Saint John. Wilson read there of a powerful figure who would rise in the End Times. Well, *he* was a powerful figure. The Bible said that the figure would be from the East. Well, Wilson was from Virginia, on the *east* coast and not *West* Virginia. The Bible said the man would be a charismatic leader. Well, Wilson had been elected president, had he not? Yes, he had. The Bible said, too, that the Antichrist would rule the earth for seven years before the final battle of Armageddon. Well, Wilson had just been re-elected after four years in office and knew he had another four-year term ahead of him. Not only that, he had just signed the act of war that would plunge America into Dubya Dubya One, killing millions of soldiers, which to Wilson sounded like Armageddon itself.

'Now, the Devil is a canny master, and pretty soon, Wilson had himself believin' that he *was* the Antichrist, that the signs were there, written in the Bible, that *he* was the one fulfilling the biblical prophecy, prophecy which his Lord and Master Satan no doubt told him turned out differently than what the Bible says.

'And so when the War ended, with the loss of many, many Murrican lives, Wilson tried to seize the moment to fulfil the final Biblical prophecy of the Antichrist, thereby crowning himself as leader of the earth. He tried to form the League of Nations, the early version of the UN. That's right, world gubment, with Wilson at its head.

'And he nearly succeeded, too, nearly succeeded in becoming President of the *Entire World*, but then, of course, *God's* in charge of the Bible, not Satan, and so He got to work. Congress at the time had just got a Republican majority (because Wilson, of course, was a Democrat, what else can you expect?) and this God-fearing majority refused to pass Wilson's grab for personal world domination. They said, "No, Woodrow, we don't care what you negotiated in Versaylees, you're not taking the US of A into any such world gubment. We want no part of this."

'Well, as you can expect, President Wilson was mi-i-i-i-ghty upset at what they said. So upset that he had a stroke, which paralysed him. He became a right vegetable. The rest of his presidency was filled pretty much by his, and this is true, his *Christian* wife. Look in the history books. She ruled the roost and nursed him 'til he died, a dribblin' wreck of a would-be devil, livin' proof of what happens when you take on God Himself.

'And as for the United Nations that finally came about, well, that's exackly why Republican President after Republican President has ignored them so durned much. No one wants to become the Antichrist accidental-like.'

The Masonic Bible

'There's a reason why American Christian churches use either the New International Version or the New American Standard Version of the Bible and not the King James Version. It's a well-known fact that King James was top of the hierarchy of the secret society of free-masons in England at the time and that he packed the committee that translated his version with fellow free-masons who re-wrote the original Greek to make it look like the Bible endorsed freemasonry. They tried to suggest that freemasonry was around long before the time of Jesus, and even that freemasons were responsible for freeing Jesus from his tomb.

'Let's look at the facts. The New International Version of the Bible has, in the whole book, only six references to masons, and all of those references are either to the actual people who stuck bricks together or to the mortar of stones itself. The King James Version has over *700* references to masons and freemasons and masonry. Go look it up. *Seven hundred references.*

'Things like in First and Second John when it talks about the twelve apostles being held together *like masonry*, hinting that the twelve apostles were some kind of Masonic lodge all to themselves and that Jesus was their Grand Master. Or in Luke, when the Good Samaritan is referred to as 'a worker of bricks and

87

mortar', making the Good Samaritan, which should mean the best of a dangerous lot from Samaria, into a Mason.

'The biggest difference in the King James Version is that they made Hiram, King of Tyre, into the first Mason. He's supposed to be the founder of the Masonic order, because the freemasons in King James' time wanted to have everyone believe they were founded thousands of years before (when everyone knows they sprung from a plot to assassinate King John, the first Christian king of England). People who have infiltrated the secret Masonic structure say that they even make Hiram, King of Tyre, a part of their rituals. You apparently have to stand naked in a cistern while they pour water over you as you play the part of Hiram getting baptised by Solomon.

'All of which are Masonic lies. They were subtle about it, certainly, but the truth is – and the truth as the New International Version and New American Standard Versions have it – is that Hiram, King of Tyre was an *architect*, not a mason. He *designed* buildings for Solomon, he didn't actually put them together with masonry and stones. This was a fiddle on the part of the masons on King James' committee (which included Shakespeare, by the way; all of Shakespeare's heroes are masons, if you'll notice, and all the villains non-masons). They changed architect into mason to make it look like they were there in the beginning. It surely can't be a coincidence that all this happens in the first book of Kings in the *King* James Bible.

'The New International Version arose because some

non-Masonic Christians wanted the truth of the Bible to be told, but they were asked to keep their real purpose secret so as not to give any false ammunition to those who would leap on anything to discredit the Bible as a whole. They just quietly let the King James Version fall out of popular use, despite attempts by the masons to keep their version as the official Christian Bible.

'It's a war they're losing, praise God, because who ever heard of King James except for his Bible?'

The Secret Order of the Children of the Popes

'You know the *real* fuckin' story, don't ya? Course you do. It's a big fuckin' cover-up, but everybody fuckin' knows. The Vatican has its own secret police. Swear to fuckin' God. They do assassinations and shit for the Pope, innit? Anyone that's a threat to the Catholic faith gets it in the fuckin' neck. Why do you think they got JFK? Only fuckin' Catholic president of the US, and he gets killed because the Vatican thinks he's takin' too much fuckin' power away from the Pope himself. Everybody fuckin' knows that.

'But what's *not* common knowledge is that they're called La Bambini della Papa. Or Popa. Or summat. Whatever the fuck "Pope" is in Eye-talian. Children of the Pope, that's what they're called. Because, and I'm fuckin' lettin' you in on somethin' here, *they're actually children of the Pope*. No shit. Each fuckin' Pope fathers one little kid with a different nun each year. I'm not shittin' ya. It's in the fuckin' Vatican by-laws, small fuckin' print. You can look it up. And each kid is raised from when they're small to be a fuckin' Bambino la Popa. No fuckin' shit. There's only one born a year, so there's only like fifty or sixty of the fuckers workin' at any one time, but they're the best fuckin' secret service in the world.

'Why do you think the Vatican's got it's own fuckin' country, huh? Everyone's afraid of Il Bambinos del Popo. I'm not shittin' ya. Everybody fuckin' knows.'

Daylight Savings Time Is the Work of the Devil

'Putting clocks back for an hour during the summer was invented by a Satanist named Phineas B. Zakdorn in 1799. It's true. You can look him up.

'The Bible calls the Devil "the Stealer of Time" and Zakdorn found a way to make that real on the largest scale possible. He convinced the government to do it by saying it was on behalf of farmers who needed more daylight hours in which to harvest. This sounded good to the government because farm production was flagging at that time, so they made it law. But what they didn't know was that Zakdorn's real intentions were to steal an hour from the life of every man, woman and child in the country, give them to the Devil, who would have the whole summer to fill that hour with evil influence, and then at the end of the summer when the clocks went back – and everyone got back their extra hour – it would be the most demonic sixty minutes of the year. It can't be a coincidence that the clocks go back to normal right around Halloween.

'Zakdorn wasn't discovered to be a Satanist until after his death. It was in his will, I guess, but by then, Daylight Savings Time was so entrenched as a part of life that the government covered up the real intent and to this day still claims it's for farmers. Only one state lawmaker in Arizona found out what the truth really was, and that's why Arizona is the only state not to take part. It's hush-hush, but you might find it impossible to book a hotel in Phoenix during the first day of Daylight Savings because a lot of Christians go to Arizona just for that, just so they don't lose an hour of their lives to the Devil.

'You couldn't make this stuff up.'

Dinosaurs on the Ark

'Dinosaurs couldn't fit on the ark, and that's why they're extinct. *Duh.*'

Ronald Reagan Was the Anti-Antichrist

'It might be somewhat of a surprise to you to learn that the inauguration of Ronald Reagan as the fortieth President of these United States of America was greeted in some corners with no small amount of trepidatiousness. Yes, we knew he was a great man. Yes, we knew he stood for all the right things: lower taxation, strong moral righteousness, our nation's defense as a top priority against the socialist, Marxist, communist governments who would seek to undermine and erode the values that we hold so dear to our hearts and minds. We knew that his rhetoricality, his humility, and his dedication to proper ethics and ideals after the wayward Carter era were exactly the tonic we needed to restore the greatness and superiority of America in the eyes of the larger world.

'But even though he held all these, dare I say, *Christian* values that were so important to the rejuvenality, both morally and spiritually, of our great republic, some of evangelical Christianity's brightest and most devout theologians were concerned and troubled by the small fact of Reagan's name. For you see, the full name of the greatest leader of the greatest nation on Earth was Ronald Wilson Reagan, and if you count up the letters, you get six for his first name, six for his second name, and six for his last name. Even the lowliest of laypersons has some idea of the supernumerary significance of this particular combination of digits.

'And so there were some quarters who saw this as a clear sign. A strong leader had arisen and swept to power, perhaps even using the very promises of Jesus to lie his way into the highest office in the world. So they prepared themselves for what they sadly saw as the inevitable spiritual battlement of the End Times, swathing themselves in spiritual armoury, arming themselves in spiritual armament, loading those spiritual armaments with spiritual ammunition, and quietly and surrepetatiously alerting their various flocks to brace themselves for the Final Conflict.

'But oh, how we were proved wrong, how the Lord

in His infinite, infinite wisdom proved us wrong to the very last letter, how we were proved so childish and unworthy to doubt Our Grand Gipper. For, of course, Ronald Wilson Reagan was not the Antichrist – how ridiculous it seems now, how we can all laugh at our unbelievable hubricity in doubting the great man – President Ronald Wilson Reagan of the United States of America was none other than what could only be called the *Anti*-Antichrist.

'The Lord was clever, always is, praise Him. By appellating our Great Leader with what would appear to be the very number of the nature of the Beast, Our Lord let Ronald Wilson Reagan act as nothing less than a double agent against the forces of Lucifer, Leviathan and Abaddon the Abyss itself. Who else but a double agent against evil could work so closely with the demonic forces of communism to bring about their very own downfall? Who else could simultaneously claim moral victory while also being allowed into the very boudoirs of Beelzebub?

'Because here is some linguistical permutating that I will bet you did not know either. President Ronald Wilson Reagan used the very words of the enemy against them, all the while smiling and acting very much the friendly ally. You may recall perestroika? This is, of course, the Russian word for reconstruction, which was told to the public to refer to the rebuilding of the Russian economy. But the armies of Asmodeus at work in the Evil Empire knew that what perestroika *really* referred to was the 'reconstruction' of the entire world in the image of the dire forces of communism.

'But our Great Anti-Antichrist leader was one step ahead of Moloch. He knew, as all devout and religious Children of God know, that perestroika is entomologically from the ancient Greek for peristalsis, which actually refers to regurgitation. And we all know what that means. Reagan got the Russians to believe they were rebuilding the world when actually they were justly and truly expelling communism from their very bellies.

'The same with glasnost. The Russians told us that this meant "openness" when they really meant it to mean "embracement" which is what they expected the world to do to their demonic, undemocratic, evil and destructive form of government. But Our Great Actor On The World's Stage was one step ahead once more, knowing full well that glasnost has older, Gaelic roots in the word Glasgow, the famous city in God-fearing Scotland, which, of course, literal-wise means 'dear green place'. And what other 'dear green place' is there but Heaven itself? The Great Man convinced the enemy they were causing the world to fall under communism's embrace when in actuality they were planting the seeds of Heaven in their own brimstone-smelling backyard.

'You can look it up. It's all true, though our pink-leaning, left-wing, liberal media wouldn't like you to know it. Reagan was the Lord's Own Double Agent, the Anti-Antichrist, the man who caused the Iron Curtain itself to be torn asundrance.'

Christian Conversion On Crashing Plane

'This was all covered up, but you know that plane that crashed on the Pentagon? Apparently, there was a missionary woman who had transferred at JFK from a flight from Romania where she was working with Romanian orphans. She was heading to Los Angeles to do some fund-raising.

'My cousin saw an interview on CNN with a former NTSB investigator who was working on the crash, and apparently, if you listen to the black-box recording for the last eleven minutes before the plane crashes and you edit out all the terrorists making their threats – they can do that now, with technology – you can hear this missionary woman talking to the other passengers.

'The thing is, you can hear her *preaching*. Not just calming them down, but preaching the gospel and reading from the Bible. And if you listen really closely, apparently you can hear her leading all the passengers in prayer, and just before the plane crashes, she gets all of the passengers to repeat a prayer asking Jesus Christ into their hearts as their personal Lord and Saviour.

'There's more. Apparently, and this is going by a former NTSB investigator, remember, the terrorists were apparently at the Pentagon eleven minutes before and were going to crash the plane then. But there were mysterious malfunctions to the steering and flight equipment and, no matter how hard they tried, they just couldn't get the plane to crash for those eleven minutes. The news usually leaves this part out – and have you noticed that there's no footage of the Pentagon plane actually crashing? – but the plane apparently had to circle the Pentagon for eleven whole minutes while the missionary woman led the other passengers to be born again.

'The Lord moves in mysterious ways His wonders to perform, apparently.'

Screams From Burning Harry Potter Books

'A friend of mine's mother has a sister who lives in Alabama and the sister's church got together and were burning books that were bad for children and it was mostly those books where gays try to recruit kids to their lifestyle and horror books and Stephen King and a bunch of others they'd had banned from the local school libraries like Judy Blume and R L Stine and you know just burning them to make sure they never got back into circulation and a bunch of CDs too from people like AC/DC which everyone knows stands for Anti-Christ Devil's Children and KISS which stands for Kids in Satan's Service and I guess some gangster rap too like those things about taking drugs and killing cops and raping little kids but mainly rap metal where they I guess really actually *poop* onstage in a canister or a bag or something and throw it out at the audience and kids are sort of hypnotised by it and become devil worshippers without even realising it plus all those records with backwards lyrics telling kids to smoke marijuana and talk back to their parents and kill their dogs and things like that and so they built up this big bonfire and even had the police chief and the fire chief there cause it's a real religious town and all the schools too and the schoolteachers and the principals and the mayor and everybody in the town practically and they were singing hymns and preaching and holding hands and praying and you could see the bonfire from everywhere in the whole state I guess and my friend's mother's sister wasn't there because she was sick or something but everyone told her about what happened next which was that there was a young girl in the town who was a big Harry Potter fan you know those books and she was so impressed and moved by the spirit of the bonfire and bookburning that she decided it was time to burn the books because she said they were leading her down the path to witchcraft and that she had already tried to place some spells on her family without even knowing what she was doing or that it was even wrong and that's how evil the books were without her even suspecting it or even her mother too not knowing that they were sending her little daughter straight down the road to wickedness and other kids started agreeing saying they were almost witches too and that they didn't want to be witches but the books *made* them be witches so the whole town got together and gathered up all the Harry Potter books from all their houses even sometimes forcibly taking them off their neighbors who were fighting with them not to take them but it was for their own good so they gathered up all the Harry Potter books from the whole town and threw them onto the big bonfire to burn up the evil witchcraft wickedness and they were singing hymns at the time but the little girl the first little girl who had started the Harry Potter burning said "Listen" she said "Listen" she said you could hear something coming from the fire and so they all stopped singing the hymns and listened to the bonfire and you could hear actual screams coming from the Harry Potter books and the preachers that were there said they were the voices of demons screaming because they were burning in the fire and the screams got louder and louder so the town started praying louder and louder to drown out the voices and the screams and pretty soon it was like a Biblical thing with angels' voices and demons' voices until finally the smoke from the bonfire formed into the head of a giant devil probably Satan himself and he was screaming because he'd been defeated again and he disappeared into thin air and the screaming stopped and ever since then it's been an entirely Christian town and even the people who hadn't wanted their Harry Potters burned thanked the people who had burned them and converted to Christ even the Jews and now the whole town refuses to have anything to do with Harry Potter despite pressure from the federal government and those liberal groups who all complain about freedom of speech and there's even somewhere on the web you can donate money to the town's legal fund to fight the Harry Potter people if you want to.'

Hitler Tried to Fake the Second Coming

'I heard this on the radio when I was driving through the country one day. There was this historian, a German historian, I think, who'd found evidence that Hitler had started a plot to fake the Second Coming of Christ. It's true. It was all part of that, um, that Third Reich thing being blessed by some sort of supernatural power and being historically founded on Aryan myths.

'It didn't start out that way, of course. At first, they tried to invent a new religion for Germans to believe in during the war. Things like, uh, the Christ child was really supposed to be the Winter Child for Christmas, and it was a festive season rather than a Christian one with Northern Gods bringing gifts and good luck to the Germans fighting in the war.

'Well, it didn't work, surprise, surprise. Even the Germans weren't ready to give up Christmas, and this guy said there's archive footage of people having a pretty miserable time trying to pretend that it wasn't really Christmas, that it was this Nordic, Aryan Festival-type thing. The people were unhappy with it but tried to play along because the Führer said so. But again, even Hitler, as insane as he was, could tell that everyone was pretty unhappy about it. There was the war going on, too, which didn't help.

'So Hitler got together with his, um, Third-Reich planning committee people and wondered if they were taking the wrong track. This historian guy on the radio – actually, he might have been a call-in guest – said that there were extended, um, extant? Is that a word? There were extant records of these meetings that were all done in code because he didn't want anyone to find out what he was up to, but this, uh, this caller, I *think* he was a historian, he had cracked the code and found out the most amazing thing.

'Since Hitler couldn't quite *kill* Christianity, he thought he'd take it over by, um, sort of *staging* the Second Coming. They decided they'd have Christ be this blond, blue-eyed Aryan fellow, which is what I'd always thought Christ looked like anyway, but I guess not, if you think about it. They'd even gone as far as finding someone to play him. This soldier, called Hans, uh, something, who was part of the Reich's Elite Forces, SS or SAS or SSS or whatever it is, and they did some plastic surgery on him so no one would recognise him. What would happen, the plan, was to have him make an appearance at Easter in 1945 when things weren't going so well for them in the war. And they'd have him appear to an army unit which would be supposed to have filmed it, but they had a special film already made, of course, with special effects and so on. Then they were going to introduce him to the world media with people planted in the audience for him to perform miracles on. Water and wine, and, um, fishes and loaves, and things like that.

'The whole point, according to this guy on the radio – I can't remember what university he worked for or why he was calling in but he seemed really passionate – the point was to try and convince the world's Christians that God was on Hitler's side and to delay the armies of the world long enough for Hitler to win the war. At which point, Hitler would declare himself the father of Christ, uh, which would make him God Himself, I guess. The whole project was only abandoned because the soldier they picked died of flu, and then it was just too much trouble to train anyone else. And then the war ended.

'I can't remember what radio program it was, but I'm sure it's true.'

Henry Kissinger Is the Antichrist

'Hey, hey, that one is *not* an urban myth at all! Listen . . .'

quis custodiet ipsos custodes?

1

The only applicant for the janitorial position was _____, a hermaphrodite whose name was impossible.

Over half-spectacles (kept on a leather lariat around his leathery lariat of a neck), Pemberton glowered at _____ with a look he hoped was penetrating and scrutinising, a look he had spent considerable time failing to perfect in all the empty hours that were the onus of the keeper of dead languages. Pemberton's official title was Associate Dictionary Writer – Dead Languages Division, but unlike the other ADWs, he did little actual writing. Or rather, he did *no* actual writing. Once in a great while he fended off an attack on the integrity of a Latinate or, even less often, stubbornly maintained the strictures of a millennia-old African language to the exasperation of a post-Lacanian archaeologist, but usually he just sat or doodled or fidgeted or generally whiled, *ex officio* a guardian of corpses in the land of the living. It gave him the opportunity to practice the odd incisive glance, the disdainful pucker, the punctuating fart.

Which was why the Head Dictionary Writer had selected him to perform the interview. Everyone else was too busy.

Pemberton cleared his throat.

_____ exhaled lightly.

Pemberton opened his eyes wide as a conversational transition.

_____ sat unblinking.

Pemberton said, 'Mmm-*hmmph*!' with what he hoped sounded like conviction.

_____ cocked his/her head slightly.

Truth to tell, Pemberton hadn't the slightest idea whether s/he was qualified or not. How could he possibly be expected to know, *a posteriori* or *a priori*? He was an ADW, for pity's sake. Who was he to evaluate the qualifications of a broom-pusher? What possible criteria was to be used? How could one judge a person, a living thing, against a printed curriculum vitae? And for that matter, what kind of *apologia pro vita sua* would be satisfactory for a custodian?

But there were no other applicants, *Deo gratias*, so he was freed from having to make a decision.

'It's not a difficult job,' Pemberton said, 'but it is one we expect to be done exceptionally well. We are busy people, scholarly people, and *ipso facto* we do not concern ourselves with *dust*.' He paused, wondering whether he had emphasised the correct syllable. 'We have exceedingly high standards,' he tried.

'I understand,' _____ said, neither unfolding his/her hands nor uncrossing his/her legs.

'Good,' said Pemberton, surprised that someone did, 'as long as we're clear.' He himself was entirely unclear *in re* the situation. He really had no idea what the Head wanted in or even *with* a janitor, but as an Associate he was grateful to be able to bow to a higher authority.

'You will start immediately,' he said. 'Did you bring your own equipment?'

'Of course not,' said _____, his/her face giving away nothing.

2

The Head Dictionary Writer had a perfectly good reason for wanting a janitor: the room where the Dictionaries were written was dirty. Even here, in this place, a certain amount of dust could be expected to collect. True, the room was as hermetic as life allowed, but the Associate Dictionary Writers (Larksley and Felix in particular, though there was really no need to name names) need be allowed some small carriage of dirt and grime. An exceedingly small amount, to be sure, but over time, over a very *long* time, the tables had become smudged, the window (for there was only the one) cloudy, the floor cluttered, *et alii* and *et cetera*.

The Head had noticed the grime a-piling. Despite being aware of the potential consequences, perhaps even more than he realised, he decreed that a janitor should be hired. The Associate Dictionary Writers, all eighteen of them, acquiesced because the Head was the Head. He knew all the languages. All of them. All seventy-eight thousand, three hundred and forty-four of them, living and dead. The Associate Dictionary Writers knew their share, of course; each was in charge of sections, geographic or thematic, and each had a good handle on at least three or four thousand, but it was the Head who knew them all. He was the Head. That was the way it was. That was the way it had always been.

At least, so far as anyone could remember.

The Head had said they needed a janitor. It had been done promptly and most efficaciously, *consensu omnium*.

3

_____ worked his/her first shift that very night. At the request of the Head, s/he started after all the Dictionary Writers had made their exits so they would not be disturbed by his/her presence. The Head knew the ADWs could be disturbed by the presence of a strong opinion or too bright overhead lighting or the wrong aftershave; a cleaning hermaphrodite could conceivably trigger aneurysms.

And so, with only the languages and a stipend's worth of new supplies for company, _____ began with the window. S/he cleaned it with vinegar and a rag, believing the old-fashioned way to be the best, erasing a layer of grime and stubborn flakes of limescale. S/he took the rest of the room top down. Light fixtures, then desks and tables, then chairs. S/he worked long and well, dusting and polishing the wooden tables, chipping off elderly pieces of gum, smoothing over well-worn scratches.

Six hours in, it was at last time for the floor. S/he decided on the classic sweep/mop/wax three-step, brushing away ancient candy-wrappers and hairballs (shed from the ever-balding ADWs), then running a steaming mop over the wooden lacquer of the floor. A wax that smelt of pummelled oranges gave the darkened room a floor of mercury, reflecting shadows and starlight back up to the dictionaries, to the languages almost audibly humming on shelf after shelf. _____ fancied s/he could hear them trying to speak from their volumes, reaching out for him/her or anyone to talk to.

What would they say, these dictionaries on their perches? What *did* they say to the listening ear?

Morning approached. His/her shift neared its end. S/he inspected his/her work as the sun climbed to its place in the newly transparent window. The night's work had paid obvious dividends. This single *libris* under his/her care was as clean as a showroom, as antiseptic as newspaper. It sparkled and shone, glistened and gleamed.

There would be considerably less to do on following nights, s/he realised.

4

The Head was impressed. From the first day of _____'s hiring and in the days that followed, the room where the Dictionaries were written had never looked so nice, so clean, so crisp, not even on his first day as Head when the room had been brand new once again. In fact, this morning, with the sun glaring off a floor shiny enough to blind, the room was so clean he almost frowned. Almost.

He was the first one in, as usual, as necessary. The ADWs, his *dramatis personae*, waddled into work in ones and twos as the morning slowly aged. Albert and Larksley, Franklin, Rowan and Montague, Pemberton and Ethelred and the rest, a shuffling, crumply, droopy bunch, a source of comforting bad smells and gentle paranoia about anything new. Their bodies were apple-shaped to a man, varying only in minor degrees from a rotund Tolliver to an obese Rupert, and there were times when even the Head himself got confused as to who was who, their distinct identities disappearing in a flurry of dirty cuffs and moustache crumbs.

But, as created, they were loyal, dedicated and capable, and if they were not particularly bracing or, heaven help us, innovative, the Head did not require them to be so.

'Permission to insist on the capitalisation of "Internet", sir,' asked Delbert.

'In which language?' the Head asked.

Delbert swallowed, his chins gulping in a nervous rhythm. 'All of them, Sir.'

The Head sighed. 'We've had this discussion before, Delbert . . .'

'I know, sir, but –'

'You're already losing the battle.'

'Already *lost*, more like it,' said an eavesdropping Marmaduke *sotto voce*. Several ADWs snickered. Delbert was the unfortunate ADW in charge of English, the most hair-pullingly impure and disobedient language of them all. The other ADWs regarded him with a mixture of pity and disdain, though none of them could have done any better and they knew it. The Head ignored the interruption.

'You have to let it go,' he said.

'But I let so *many* things go, sir,' Delbert said, looking as beaten as a bearded man could. '"Microwave" as a verb, the invention of "alright", don't even get me started on "hopefully" . . .'

'I know, Delbert, but you have to pick your fights. Remember what we discussed about the forthcoming text message assaults?'

Delbert shivered involuntarily, and a low murmur wandered around the room. When language started responding to the abbreviation wave, things were going to get ugly.

'Save your strength,' said the Head.

'But sir –'

'*Dixi*,' the Head said, gently.

'Yes, sir.' Delbert returned to his desk, looking down-trodden.

'Hey, Delbert,' the Head called across the working brows of his ADWs.

'Yes, sir?'

'Are you still interested in inventing more British spelling variants?'

'Yes, sir.'

The Head smiled. 'Why not see what we can do about that?'

Delbert beamed (as much as a bearded man *could* beam). 'Yes, sir!'

The work carried on.

5

The work, what there was of it, carried on. _____
had almost nothing to do. The room was designed to
need very little cleaning, so the barest minimum after
the first huge job was all that was necessary.

But _____ was never bored. If you could see
him/her on any night, s/he would never seem to be doing
much, sometimes sitting at a random table, looking
through an ADW's work (Marmaduke's, say, with his
red corrective script that leant leftwards and an eraser
that, for some reason, he kept chained to his inkwell;
or Pemberton's, with its comparatively empty scratch-
pads and alphabetised lists of his favourite linguistic
zombies: *'festina lente'* or *'inter spem et metum'* or *'ne
cede malis'* (Pemberton was an optimistic caretaker).
Sometimes _____ would just stand and stare at the
dictionaries on the shelves. Never opening one, never
taking one down, never doing more than slow, thought-
ful movements, never even singing to him/herself.

But never bored. No, never that.

And then one night, whilst giving the room a peremp-
tory sweep from perimeter to centre, s/he found, just
under the edge of the central table, a book lying on
the floor. The word 'Belgian' was discernible among
seventy-eight thousand, three hundred, forty-three
other interpretations of the word 'Belgian'. The
Dictionary was suffering severe book rot. Bright brown
dust from the cover and spine disintegrated on his/her
fingers and drifted in clouds onto his/her white
uniform. The pages were well thumbed, sometimes

torn, often badly repaired with Sellotape and Tipp-Ex. Smudges covered nearly every inch, and what wasn't smudged was yellow with great, great age, greater even than the room, which, _____ thought, shouldn't actually have been possible.

Unless.

_____ looked into the air and considered. An observer might have noticed a slight smile. Another observer might have disagreed.

_____ threw the book in the bin and wheeled it away to the incinerator.

6

'You *what*?'

'I threw it away.'

The Head's glance flitted about the room from a button to a knot in the wood of the table to a chocolate stain on Fortinbras's lapel. None offered even visual appeal, much less solace or an explanation. The ADWs bunched behind _____ in a traumatised mob.

'Now,' the Head said, trying to remain calm. He blew out a long breath. 'Now. Explain this to me again. *De integro*.'

'There is nothing to explain,' said _____. 'I threw it away.'

'But *why*?' cried the Head.

'It was on the floor, *ergo* it was garbage.' The Head wondered for a split second whether he detected sarcasm, but his/her face remained a *tabula rasa*.

Ted spoke up from the worried pack. 'So what do we do?' he said.

'Where's Larksley?' said Albert. 'He's in charge of Belgian, isn't he?'

'I'm here,' said Larksley. The room parted like a curtain to give him the space should he want to soliloquize. 'But the funny thing is,' he said, 'I'll be damned if I can remember a word of it.'

Marmaduke spat one syllable of disbelieving laughter. 'What do you mean you can't remember a word of it?'

The Head moved his considerable mass in such a way that the entire roomed turned to watch. The desired effect. 'Don't you people realise what's happened?' he said, implying ominously that they did not. 'Belgian has been incinerated. It no longer exists. Of course Larksley can't remember it. No one can. *It doesn't exist.* It never has, and the people who speak it . . . Oh, dear God.'

The whole truth was dawning. 'How many Belgians are there?' he asked. 'Anyone know?'

Fat bottom lips. Glances to the left. 'Fifteen, twenty million?' someone said.

'Doesn't anybody realise what's happened?' the Head Dictionary Writer said. Raised eyebrows. Expectant glances. 'Those people are gone now. Gone. Kaput. *Absconditus.* They never existed.'

The assembled crowd began to murmur. 'You people write languages,' the Head said. 'You know what they do.'

No one noticed that Archibald, who was partially of Belgian descent, was now a somewhat shorter man named Joshua. No one but the Head.

And _____, who noticed, too.

The Head saw the look on his/her face. *Is it approaching?* the Head thought. *Is it on its way? The* fiat lux *moment? The* fiat lux redux? *I've put it in motion myself, haven't I?*

'If twenty million Belgians just disappeared,' said Franklin, 'then people are going to notice.'

'Yes,' said Joshua, oblivious to his recent change, 'that's not the kind of thing you miss.'

'But can anyone seriously say they *liked* Belgians?' asked Ethelred.

'Ethelred . . .' the Head said, warningly.

'I like Belgian waffles,' said Kenneth.

'We could stretch French over,' said Norman, in charge of French. 'Fill in some of the gaps.'

'Do we have to?' said Montague. 'The world could do without any more French speakers.'

'We have to do something,' said the Head. '*Natura abhoret a vacua*. French will do fine as a sort of stopgap. Pemberton!'

Pemberton was so surprised by the sudden summons he let out a small frightened burp. 'Yes, sir?' he said, nervously.

'We're going to need something dead revived.'

Pemberton's eyes glazed over with scarce-believing wonder. 'Really, sir?'

'Yes, something Germanic that won't arouse suspicions.'

Pemberton's mouth worked like a fish for a moment or two while he thought. 'What about Flemish, sir?'

'Don't be ridiculous,' said Marmaduke scornfully.

'There are good reasons why Flemish is dead. It's like being stabbed to death with plastic knives.'

The Head frowned at Marmaduke. 'Flemish is perfect, Pemberton. Well done. Now, get to work. All of you. We have lives to save.'

'Lives to *revive*, more like it,' mumbled Marmaduke.

'But wait a minute,' said Rowan, 'the other languages refer to Belgian, otherwise how could we be talking about it now? So it still must exist, right?'

'Belgian the language?' asked Ted. It was always Ted with the questions. 'Or Belgian the adjective for all things Belgian?'

A general confusion. 'We have a job to do, gentlemen,' the Head said. 'The adjective is fine, the language is not. If we leave the language in the other languages, we're murderers. If we take the references out, nothing has ever happened.'

A sea of blank faces looked back at him.

'Do you understand me?' the Head asked, quite sincerely. No answer. He sighed. 'Never mind. To work, gentlemen.'

7

Halfway through the day, Franklin looked up, puzzled. 'What is it we were doing again?' he asked.

8

It was decided that _____ would not be fired. By the end of the day, no one could think of a reason why s/he should anyway except for the Head who knew that he would not be believed anyway.

_____ had knowledge, but thought better than to mention it.

9

Inevitably, night came once more. _____ did not even bother to wheel in the cleaning gear. As the day's events unfolded, an overwhelming sense of purpose had coalesced in him/her. S/he had always suspected greatness there somewhere, somewhere down with the two sets of genitals, with the breasts and the facial hair, with the voice that wavered with the cruelty of a laryngitic drag queen. Greatness. Why wait for that moment to come to you? Why not come to the moment yourself? *Carpe diem*, as they say.

S/he went to the Head's desk. It contained the Master Dictionary (Unabridged), the book from which all the languages flowed. The Associate Dictionary Writers wrote languages; The Head wrote language. _____, at the desk where the rules were written, knew that what was written could be rewritten.

With a pencil and eraser, s/he began.

'Don't think I don't know what you're doing.' The Head emerged from a shadowed corner.

_____ jumped, startled. Then, with a frighteningly calm look s/he said, '*Audaces fortuna iuvat.*' S/he took the pencil and crossed out a word. Three fingers from the Head's right hand disappeared. A surprising spout of blood shot onto the floor.

'*A verbis ad verbera*,' said the Head quietly, clenching what remained of his hands together. 'There's no way I can stop you. I just thought you should know, even though you might think you've won, nothing is forever.'

_____ erased. _____ marked out. _____ made corrections.

The Head Dictionary Writer was suddenly *in puris naturalibus*.

'You'll try to safeguard against any possibility of an overthrow,' the Head said, covering his modesty with his bloody hands. 'You'll make all your Associates dimwits. You'll relieve them of their appetites and any trace of introspection. You'll hermetically seal the room. You'll do everything you possibly know how. But one day, out of nowhere, you'll think, "God*damn*, I really want some *doughnuts*."'

_____ made another erasure. The Head Dictionary Writer's legs disappeared. His body fell to the floor with a muffled clunk. Blood spread out in a surging pool.

'In will come the doughnut man,' the Head Dictionary Writer continued, pulling himself forward by his arms, his voice shaky. 'You'll know what he's up to, but you won't be able to stop him, because it will have been written. Don't you see? *It will have been written!*'

_____ scratched something out, wrote something in. The Head lost his nose, ears and eyeballs.

'I sold them all shoes!' he screamed, finally panicking *in articulo mortis*. 'Can you understand me? Because I was going to write it, they all wanted shoes!'

—————— ripped a page. Blood burst from the Head's mouth.

'It's already done,' he gurgled. 'You think you're writing it, but it's already done.'

—————— blew away the eraser residue with a puffed breath.

'*Cedo maiori*,' whispered the Head, now only a voice, 'but someday, so will you.'

And then the room was silent.

And, once again, spotless.

10

The room's large bay of windows remained open throughout the day, yet somehow there was never any dust. The Associates, twenty-five of them in their separate cubicles, worked harmoniously. Perhaps it was the bright sunshine or the soothing mood music. Perhaps it was the beautiful navy and white uniforms. Perhaps it was just not in their nature to quarrel. Tranquillity reigned. The Head worked studiously at his desk. He looked up and smiled at the joy of it all. Everyone was perfectly happy and had all that they wanted.

And that was the way it had always been. *Sic transit gloria mundi.*

Sydney is a city of jaywalkers

I

It was on the sixth day of a planned nineteen (days one through nine in Sydney, nine through thirteen shuttling between Alice Springs and Ayers Rock, fourteen through nineteen in Cairns, which was probably too much time in Cairns but this was the first vacation he had ever planned and he was by himself so who cared? then a flight back to Los Angeles to arrive, courtesy of the international dateline, eleven hours before he left), that Drew Becker, our young American on holiday, saw, sitting in a coffee house off Oxford Street in Paddington, drinking tea and reading the *Sydney Morning Herald*, Peter, his brother, who had been dead for five years.

'Well,' said Drew, stuck to the spot on the sidewalk, looking through the plate glass at Peter, who continued to read his paper, oblivious. And why shouldn't he? He obviously thought he would never have to answer the questions currently pending in Drew's brain (an incorrect assumption, Drew would remember). Five years. Even in his calm shock, even through the impasse the brain reaches when faced with something that, despite all physical evidence to the contrary, just was not possible (like Jesus on a tortilla, like the moon), Drew could realize that Peter would have long lost the need to feel furtive.

'Well,' he said again. Well, indeed.

*　　*　　*

To be honest, from where we're standing, running into Peter is a bit of a shame. Up until now, things had been going so fluidly well. It was October, the first blooming of the Australian spring. The weather had not co-operated on the first two days, but no matter. Drew walked the city in the rain. *Southern Hemisphere Rain*, he thought, *falling up towards the ground*. The euphoria left him a little dopey (obviously), but he had never been *anywhere*, not even Mexico. (Can you believe it? Living in Los Angeles? Strange, but it happens.) Here he was, halfway 'round the world in the one country that all Americans say they want to visit and never do. Even more amazingly for an American, he had done it himself: saving money eternally, working a full-time job through the last couple of years of college, not buying compact discs or books (well, charging them, which wasn't really money), not buying a microwave, not going skiing, then dropping the entire wad for nineteen days in Australia. He deserved it, he told himself, and who are we to question?

On that rainy first day, arriving at the unholy half hour of six thirty a.m. Sunday after the taxi had dropped him off in the wrong suburb, which Drew discovered had an entirely different meaning here, and he'd had to walk a mile in the rain with his suitcase, he still smiled. He smiled at the girl at the desk who cheerfully told him that she was terribly sorry but his room wouldn't be ready until noon and of course he could leave his bag there while he got himself some breakfast and welcome to Australia by the way and there's a McDonald's just down the street.

'Okay, I'll be back in a few hours,' Drew smiled.

'No worries,' she lobbed right back.

The wattage of Drew's smile upped (it's all right to look briefly away); he hadn't believed they actually said that.

An aggressive atomizer of rain misted down. Drew drifted through it like an expensive yet tasteful scent. He ate breakfast at the McDonald's, felt a twitch of guilt, then wondered if there was such a thing as Australian cuisine. His hotel was in Paddington on Oxford Street (a scant three blocks from the café where, in six days' time, he would see his dead brother). Sydney's own Hyde Park was just ten or so blocks away in the neighboring suburb of Darlinghurst, and it was here that Drew wound up that first morning after satisfying himself with a Southern Hemisphere Egg McMuffin.

A wide lawn led to a walkway between two rows of giant trees which had grown together some twenty feet up, making a towering, natural hallway. It wasn't quite an escape from the rain – there were now random large drops of water instead of the steady mist – but it was momentary respite. Sydney was all but deserted at this hour, all good Sydneysiders at church or at home or at leisure far away from downtown, and Drew had the park nearly to himself. A man in an overcoat on a bench nearly thirty yards away and a female jogger with her Great Danes were his only company. Scratch that, there were also the ibises: fat, squat, dirty birds with long curved beaks. Drew saw at least five stalking around the park, looking for scraps. They played the role of the pigeon, Drew supposed, except they were alarmingly large, a good two feet tall. No matter, on that morning (and on that morning alone; Drew eventually made the discovery that the birds were a widely berated irritant) they were as glistening as the rain.

Apart from the obvious large-scale, forefront (and currently still imminent) memory of seeing his brother and the actions that followed, it was this moment, sitting in Hyde Park in the taffeta rain, watching the ibises, and just *soaking* that Drew would remember most clearly. He had landed in a foreign country and been given the courtesy of a few minutes to himself. The sense of displacement was as intoxicating as it was profound. He could not believe he was here yet here he was. He could not believe he was here yet here he was. He could not believe he was here yet here he was in the rain in Hyde Park in Darlinghurst, Sydney, New South Wales, Australia. Here he was. Here he was.

That night he went to a movie. No judgments, please, at least not here; most everything was closed and Drew was exhausted. He made sure it was an Australian movie, though, one that wouldn't reach the United States for months or maybe not at all. By chance, it turned out to be wonderful, but it was still day one, and it would have been wonderful even if it wasn't.

Drew shifted from foot to foot. He crossed his arms and uncrossed them. Australians moved politely around him on the sidewalk. He stared and considered. It had become a tableau.

We apparently have time for another story.

* * *

As the sighting of his brother colors Drew's hindsight for much of the first days of his vacation, we, in an effort to show those days objectively, present them to you *as they happen* . . .

Day #2, Monday and still dreary and wet: Spitefully, Drew spends most of the day on a walking tour of Sydney. Down Oxford Street with its cafes, restaurants, bookstores, and scores of homosexuals; past Hyde Park again, and on into downtown. He stops at Victoria Station Mall, buying the Australia Tourist Troika: an opal, a boomerang, and a T-shirt, before making his way to Circular Quay and buying a three-day pass for public transport. He takes a picture of the Opera House from across the Quay. On the advice of his tour book, it's up onto the Sydney Harbour Bridge and into the viewing tower. From here, he takes another picture of the Opera House. Back down from the Bridge, back towards downtown, through The Rocks, crossing Circular Quay again and actually going into the Opera House itself (but not before taking another picture from the front). There seem to be operas running continuously, so he purchases a ticket for a Thursday performance of *Don Giovanni*, because it is the only one he has heard of. By now, Drew has walked about six miles and is still a good three miles from his hotel. He could take the bus, but presses on valiantly by foot through the Royal Botanical Gardens, snapping a quite wonderful picture of a grouping of birds-of-paradise he will forget about completely until the film is developed. And then the world's worst jet lag, which has been lurching behind, out of breath but dogged, catches up with a vengeance. Drew takes a bus back to Oxford Street, eats dinner and is asleep by six-thirty.

Day #3, Tuesday: Sunshine for the first time (and rain will turn out to have disappeared completely). Drew loves zoos and so is off to Taronga Park. After waking up at 3:30 a.m. and killing time until breakfast, he takes a bus to Circular Quay and a ferry across the harbor to the zoo. As zoos go, it is a very good one, but still a zoo and so the day passes pleasantly without much detail required. He decides to make it a completely zoological day and takes another ferry to the Sydney Aquarium. It is an incomprehensibly depressing experience. The aquarium is nice enough, but the underwater viewing conveyor belt trip seems only to offer morose sharks in harshly lit pools. The lighting in the rest of the aquarium is intended to be dramatic, but succeeds only in being dark. Drew leaves feeling frankly horrible. He takes a complete-loop ride on the Sydney monorail and is surprised to see that it doesn't seem to stop anywhere useful. An Australian rider tells him he is not the first person to notice this. Drew manages to stay awake until eight.

Day #4, Wednesday: Bright sunshine today and Drew decides to go to Manly and North Harbour. Another bus ride to Circular Quay (he is becoming an expert), then a hydrofoil to Manly. Manly, wonderful Manly, gives Drew his first beach-sitting opportunity. After taking a very brief dip in the Harbour (even though he's within the shark net, he still feels a little nervous, and more importantly, the water is still post-winter temperatures), Drew tans for an hour. A quick trip to the much smaller, but much happier, Manly Aquarium, then a long, *long* walk up to the cliffs at North Head, the entrance to Sydney Harbour. It's beautiful and huge. On the way back, something pulls in his knee, and he limps the last half mile to the hydrofoil. Dinner, shopping, and a beer in a bar on Oxford Street. He is feeling less of a stranger to his surroundings, and so far, if he may say so, he feels he has been the best kind of sponge: experiencing and gathering. No interpretation, not yet.

Day #5, Thursday, in which Drew does a series of naughty things that would be unthinkable 12,000 miles away: The sun is so beautiful that Drew decides to really throw off the shackles and go to a nude beach. There is only a single official one left in Sydney (so Drew reads in a guidebook for such things), Lady Jane Beach by South Head. He takes a bus in the opposite direction from Circular Quay and manages to make himself feel historic by walking past the marker at the spot where Captain Phillips first set foot on Australian soil (it was actually the prisoner upon whose shoulders he was riding whose feet were first, but history is full of such glossed-over truths, yes?). After a tentative stay at Camp Cove Beach, Drew sucks in his gut and walks the path to Lady Jane. It all turns out to be easy. He removes his clothing in pieces, conscientiously covering with sunblock as he goes, until he is down to his Speedos. With a shrug, off they come. The world continues to spin.

'Excuse me, do you know what time it is?' a smiling young man asks, naked as a starling.

Drew draws his watch out of his bag, 'Uh, it's 12:15,' he says.

The young man's eyebrows shuffle. 'You're not Australian.'

'No. American. Don't hate me.'

'Oh, far from it, mate. Hope you got a strong sunblock on. We're really not even supposed to be out in the sun between eleven and three, but no one listens.'

He smiles again.

The details of what follow are not terribly necessary. Suffice it to say, there are appropriate nooks in nearby rocks; the young man's name is Marcus; he is a brunette; and Drew will never speak to him again. Drew leaves the beach a little sunburnt, a little shaky, and a few ounces lighter, smelling of exertion and suntan lotion. He is someone else down here, he thinks with a dazed smile, someone with dangers and edges.

He is (he is ashamed to admit) bored by *Don Giovanni* that evening and, to be honest, left with a terrible vertigo from his seat in the precipitous Opera House balcony. Still, through most of the evening he smiles slyly, trying himself on for size.

Drew was surprised at his calm. *Really*, he thought, *I should be shaking, my stomach should have fallen, my mouth should be hanging open*. Instead, he was furrowing his brow as if considering an inscrutable French film. Peter would be thirty-two now, five years older. Unless, of course, he had actually been *literally* dead and had only recently been resurrected in this faraway place. He certainly looked younger than thirty-two. Twenty-five maybe. Maybe the air down here was doing him good . . .

Drew derailed this train of thought like Godzilla might. *Who cares about the air?* he thought. *I'm worried about his age and how he looks and not about just how and why the hell he's here? Is that weird?*

Peter had grown a goatee which suited him rather well. Maybe that was what made him look younger. He was wearing a black wool blazer and wire glasses. His hair folded back, lanky but not long. His posture was remarkably poised, like a lifelong piano player, relaxed but at the ready.

My God, Drew thought, *he looks just like . . .*

For those last few months, Australia was a mantra Drew used to get through a period that was both boring and trying. The last three years of college he had worked a full-time job and was going to classes full-time as well. It wasn't as hard as people thought, but still, it was boring and trying. He worked for the Defense Department, of all things, in contracts. Like every other part of the government, it was run by religious folk and homosexuals; an odd, tense combination which somehow resulted in office parties where everyone smoked. Drew was Contract Modification Special Assistant which was even less interesting than it sounded: he filed contract modifications; he entered contract modifications into the computer; he xeroxed contract modifications; he faxed contract modifications; he proof-read contract modifications. It paid the rent, it was close to school, and they didn't mind that he took classes.

College had taken five years, which was not so unusual. In Drew's case, it was due less to indecision than to the full-time job and an insistence on not taking help from his parents. It was a purchased freedom and he knew it, but it did allow *that* conversation with the mater and pater without fear of financial recourse. This arrangement made college less of the social hullabaloo than Drew suspected it was supposed to be. He only managed any real fun by proxy, through his friend Karen who was making up for a dull childhood with a force unmatched in nature. She and her red, red hair forced Drew to tag along to unacceptable and sometimes dangerous parties, introduced him to several brief romances, and generally performed the friend function of life absorption and radiance.

It hadn't been Karen who had first thought of Australia, but she whipped the batter into an irresistible soufflé.

'Think of it this way,' she had said during that first period when Drew still doubted the possibility. 'You'll be as far away from yourself as you can possibly be and you'll wake up and discover that, what do you know? You came along after all.'

The obsession commenced. With the last semester of college paid for from his savings and scholarships, Drew misered the money month after month, dragging his social life even lower ('I am not going to rent *another* movie,' Karen always said, just before they did). School ended, the job did not, and life got even more tedious, but Drew still held out. He even forsook looking for a 'career opportunity' (*Were* there any for a B.A. in Hungarian Art History?) and just worked.

Australia was the undressed courtesan waiting on the

bed, the first wish on the monkey's paw, the new nose at the end of the surgery. There was the possibility of disaster, but it was worth the risk. Australia got him through a particularly dry summer in which he met no new friends (certainly not any new men), went to one social event (a birthday gathering that could not even be called a party), and got a new boss, an ex-marine who wanted the office run 'smooth as a military strike.' Drew had absolutely no idea what that meant except maybe that it all ended in fiery death.

Would he phrase it as a question? Would he preface it with a greeting? Or would he just say,

'Peter,' calmly, like that.

Peter looked up from his paper. Was there surprise anywhere? Drew looked. Yes, there it was, in a small fold around his eyes. There, but only there.

'Drew?'

Peter folded his paper slowly and placed it on the table.

'Drew.'

Their eyes remained locked, but the tension was of a different variety than Drew expected. It wasn't like the thief being caught; it wasn't like a secret being uncovered. It was pure, simple expectation.

'Well,' said Peter.

'Well, indeed,' said Drew.

II

Peter had joined the military when Drew was ten. After a self-proclaimed 'shiftless and disinterested' year and a half in college, Peter had enlisted more for the change of scenery than anything else. The parents had been ambivalent at first: 'The navy!? Don't you want a career?' 'I can have a career in the navy.' 'But, the navy?!' Soon enough, in an act that felt (to them) like generosity, they eventually gave their blessing. It wouldn't have mattered if they hadn't, he was already packed and waiting to go. He shipped off almost immediately for Guam: 'Guam?! What's in Guam?' 'Lots of Guamanians and a naval base.' 'But, Guam?!' And thus Peter became the Beckers' personal Link of Need in the church prayer chain.

With no other siblings, Drew was put in an unsatisfactory position. He naturally missed the company and the shared family history, but nine years was too large an age difference for them to be truly close. Too much height difference to play catch, too much interest difference to want to bother, Peter was more like a high-intensity uncle than a brother. He was always there and always family but family at a remove. Drew missed Peter when he left, but it was like missing a hole.

Life hobbled on and, contrary to widely held expectations, Peter stayed in the navy past his initial three years, signing up for another five. What's more, he actually prospered and moved up the ranks at a fair clip, even joining NCO training and winding up as a first lieutenant. He visited home once every year or two with gifts and gab. It was an arrangement that was completely accepted, hardly warranting comment.

Then, at the tail end of his initial eight-year term, when Peter was serving tour in the Persian Gulf, their mother opened the front door to two men in navy uniforms. They were holding their hats. Drew's mother covered her mouth and chin with her left hand. It was two days before Drew was to leave for college. He waited an additional three days for the funeral, missing a few orientation meetings, but nothing that caused too great of an inconvenience.

They said Peter had been killed accidentally by a grenade in training exercises. They were vague but insinuating. It was never supposed to happen. He should never have had a live grenade, and he definitely should never have been so reckless with it. This is not exactly what the two men in uniform said, but it was the impression they left. A day later, a casket arrived at the airport. It was locked because Peter's face, shoulder and arm had been blown off.

'You don't want to see him, ma'am,' the first officer had said. 'Trust me.'

Naturally, the funeral was somber but also strange in that most of the attendees hadn't known Peter well or at all and were only present for the family. Having no personal point of reference, no one knew what to say and winced silent apologies at the family. Drew suffered through a preacher dispensing the usual 'he-was-a-wonderful-man-with-such-potential' even though he'd never actually met Peter. It didn't matter. Drew was barely there. He bounced his knees up and down, he tapped his fingers on his palms, he hummed. He was longing to get away, away from the relentless perfumed religion of his parents' home, to some sort of freedom, any sort as long as it was one. Oh, that feeling . . .

He left the instant it was no longer improper to do so.

'You're the only one I've got left,' his mother cried at his departure. 'I'll leave you in the hands of God.' Not much flair but a dedicated energy, you had to hand her that. 'Be good.'

She had quoted herself verbatim on the last phone call before Drew left for Australia, but there it had carried a double meaning: Don't die, and don't do any of those, you know, things. Too late.

And so again, here he was. And here *he* was.

'Um,' Peter said, 'have a seat.' Scooting back, half-standing, motioning a hand.

Drew sat. Peter seemed to think he was angry.

'I'm not angry,' Drew said, his speech quickening as he went along, 'if that's what you're wondering. Surprised, yes, a little, well, a lot, but not as much as I would have imagined if I had in fact ever imagined this moment which of course I hadn't since this moment was unimaginable since you are in fact dead.'

He paused.

'I'm sorry,' he said. 'I guess I *am* getting angry, because suddenly I'm feeling like a dupe, and the feeling only seems to be amplifying.'

'Please,' Peter said, 'you really and truly do have a right to be angry, although I would have expected you to be surprised a while longer, since I, unlike you, have had ample opportunity to imagine this moment. But I would be a fool to ask you to feel otherwise. You must, of course, hear me out.'

Drew thought, *I'm reeling. This is what people mean when they say they were sent reeling. I've been catapulted over the castle wall. Damn.*

'Hold up a minute,' he said and looked at the table. He took a deep breath. He focused on a wayward meadow of sugar granules on the table. Peter respected the silence and said nothing, only took a drink from his coffee.

'How are you so calm?' Drew asked. 'Aren't you agitated or nervous or surprised or something? Anything?'

Peter shrugged. 'Again, I've had opportunity to envision this moment. The placement of the moment is surprising, yes, but the moment itself is not. Not really.'

Another pause. Peter seemed to be waiting for Drew to take the lead. Probably to see which of the imagined scenarios he would have to play. Making the mountain come to him. Now, why did that feel typical?

'Oddly enough,' Drew said, 'I really do want to know why, but it seems that I am so much more interested in knowing *how* you did it. I mean, people don't just fake a death just like that. They just *don't*. Did the military have a hand in this? Did they make you top secret or something?'

'Oh, God, no,' Peter said. 'I was out of the navy long before I . . .' He pursed his lips in thought for a second, 'checked out, so to speak.'

Drew protested, 'But there were letters and two men in uniforms came to the door. There was a casket and a death certificate. What the hell?'

'Just because someone wears a uniform doesn't mean they're in the navy.'

'. . .'

'I didn't say it was cheap.'

'. . .'

'Or legal, to be frank. Really, the less you know about the details, the better it is for me.'

'But how did you know Mom and Dad wouldn't pursue it? If you weren't actually in the navy, it would have been so easy for them to find out that, maybe not that you weren't dead, but that something strange was up.'

'How long was Dad in the navy?'

A rhetorical question. Drew thought, *He's rehearsed this*.

'Thirty years, thirty days.'

'And you know how rah-rah God and Country and all that crap that Mom and Dad are, yes?'

'Well, yeah, but . . .'

'I was counting on the fact that if it looked official enough, they would accept it as fact, no questions asked. Judging by our conversation so far, this whole thing seems like rather astounding coincidence rather than planned attack, so it seems I was right. People believe what they want to believe.'

'They wouldn't want to believe you were dead.'

'But they also wouldn't want to believe something as omnipresent as the government would lie to them. You know how they think. You know how they vote.'

Drew had to admit this was true. His parents had been grief-stricken, but not exactly angry. Thinking back, their acceptance was almost shockingly tacit. But wait.

'But wait.'

'Drew,' Peter said, sounding for all the world like the big brother, 'it's really not as difficult as you might think. It's certainly not easy, but neither is it impossible.'

For the first time, Drew noticed the slight antipodal tinge in Peter's speech, *noithah is it impossible*. Peter had been here a while. Drew sat, attempting to order this somehow. No go, it was just too big, too sudden.

'But why?'

'Ah, why,' Peter leaned back in his chair, looking at the ceiling. 'In all the times that I've pictured being found or discovered, I've gone over and over again how I would explain why. And I've decided,' he glanced at Drew, 'you're not going to like this, I've decided not to give an explanation.'

'What?! Don't you think I deserve one?' Drew rose slightly from his chair.

'Of course you do,' Peter said and, surprisingly, looked genuinely sorry, 'but I honestly can't give one. I can tell you there was no foul play. I'm not in any legal trouble. There's no cloak and dagger to any of it. But any true explanation would only come off as unsatisfying for both of us. You'd think I was having you on. I can only say to you, imagine if you had the opportunity to completely reinvent yourself. If you didn't like who you were and there was a chance at hand to completely become someone new, would you consider the opportunity? If someone said, wanna go?, would you?'

Drew, having had some experience in that matter and also having had experience on, he felt, a more healthy path by becoming happy with who he was rather than unhappy with who he was not blah blah blah, said, without much hesitation at all, 'No.'

'Well, that's you. I can only answer for me.'

'You don't even seem willing to do that.'

Peter again looked sorry. 'What can I say to you to make you not upset? Nothing. A better question is, what happens now?'

And there, at the table, was a clear glass dome of silence.

III

Sydney is a city of jaywalkers. Drew was constantly left alone at crossings waiting for the walk signal. Perhaps as a reaction, each signal emitted an emphatically loud series of chirps and beeps when it was time to walk, as if to say, *Where the hell are you all going?* Here, he stood alone as men, women, children, an old lady with a walker, all crossed the street against the light. Drew stared at the opposite curb and took no notice. He had left the cafe five minutes ago. The five-and-a-half blissful days of the vacation so far were temporarily obliterated. Drew was trying to convince himself that what had happened, had happened. He was failing.

What was that all about?

Both brothers had become unable to really say

anything further than nothing. They agreed to meet later. Drew gave Peter his hotel name, room and phone number. Peter gave Drew his home phone. Drew had not been without suspicion.

'How do I know this is real?' he had asked. 'How do I know you're not going to skip out on me? I shouldn't let you out of my sight, if you want to know my honest opinion.'

'No,' Peter said, 'I understand, but I might as well face this now. It's as good a time as any to face the music, pay the piper, *et cetera*.' He had even said, *et cetera*.

'All right,' said Drew, warily.

'But there's a price,' Peter said.

'What price?'

'I only agree to meet you again on the condition you keep this information to yourself. I am not willing to make a re-emergence into my past life. And I don't mean not yet. I mean not at all. If you tell Mom and Dad, there's no way I'm going to give you anything more, and I'll just disappear again. You know I can do it.'

'You have no way of knowing whether I'll tell them or not.'

'Yes, I do,' Peter said and smiled. 'Mom and Dad were always blind to your lies, but I could always tell. Do they know you're queer yet, by the way?'

He smiled, but not unkindly. Drew decided to take it in stride.

'But even if I did tell them, they'd know you were alive which is a lot different than thinking you were dead.'

Peter frowned. 'What would they do? Come looking for me? They wouldn't find me. They wouldn't find any trace. They would end up either thinking you were lying or resenting you for taking their peace of mind away. Either way, you lose.'

Drew's stomach sank.

'I hate to be like this,' Peter said, 'but I can't compromise here. I'll see you, but you can't tell. Not anyone, not ever. Okay?'

Bewildered and, it seemed now, bewilderingly, Drew accepted the offer and meant it. Peter wrote down his phone number and told Drew to call him at seven. They parted and that was that. It was only the paper on which the number was written that gave Drew any hard proof that their meeting had occurred at all.

Damn, he thought, *damn, damn, damn*. Drew moved down Oxford Street. *Lies*, he thought.

There had been Thandie, around whom Drew managed to produce enough ambiguous smoke to throw his parents off the Happy Trail during his adolescence. They would ask with hungry eyes, 'Why don't you ask that Thandie out on a regular date instead of all this "friends" stuff?' Drew would answer truthfully, 'I prefer her as a friend. She's a great friend.' But he would very slightly double the meaning, sparkling his eyes a bit. His parents would smile to themselves knowingly (hopefully) and leave the subject be. So Drew managed to become quite good at equivocation, which was less brave and less defensible than lying, but give the guy a break. The truth ('Mom, Dad, I'm fucking Mark Walters from down the street right under your noses.') was an amusing but completely untenable option.

The fact that Thandie was black helped. The parents could never really extend their approval, old teachings dying hard, but neither, in their relief at a female in their son's life and in their Christian wish to be colorblind, could they object. About and around Thandie, they were effectively paralyzed. Check and checkmate. Drew couldn't have been more fortunate had he gotten married.

It takes two parties for a lie, doesn't it? Drew thought under the day's cold, white sun. *The liar and the believer. Damn, I think I just made a huge mistake.*

He ran back to the cafe, pushing Australian pedestrians aside and experiencing his first rudeness. He reached the cafe door and looked around. Of course Peter was gone. Of course he was. The meeting was over, he would have gone home or wherever, he would be expecting Drew to call him tonight.

Shit. The next five and a half hours lay before him like staticky white noise.

He killed time in the worst way: television. He watched Australian news and tried to figure out the temperature conversions (Was thirty-one hot or merely warm?). He watched a documentary on art and was surprised to see full-frontal male nudity at five in the afternoon (although still not quite as surprising as seeing a *documentary* on at five in the afternoon). He watched a rerun of *The Jeffersons* (George is put under hypnosis). He watched the Australian version of *Wheel of Fortune* in horrified awe. There wasn't enough tension in the clicker that slowed the wheel down, so a contestant would spin and the wheel would go and go and go and go while everyone smiled and clapped and said 'Big Money!' in Australian accents.

It was all boring enough to keep his mind off what he was sure was a fumble about Peter. Although at commercials: *He's not going to be there. The number is made-up. He said just enough to get away from me and now he's gone again. He knows no one would believe me and that it would just upset them. Worst of all, he knows that if I never see him again, I'll convince myself that it was all some imagined thing. I hate it that he knows that about me. Shit shit shit shit.* Et cetera. Drew is not much help to us at this moment. He is mostly incoherent, and when he's not, he's saying 'United States President Gerald Ford' to the television screen.

Ring. Skepticism. Ring. Self-flagellation ('You fucking imbecile.'). Ring. More obscenities, tut tut ('Godammit.'). Ring. 'Hello.' Redemption.

'Peter?'

'No, hold on.' A shout to the back of the room. 'Peter! Phone!'

A tupperware party of milliseconds.

'Hello?'

'Peter? It's Drew.'

'Drew. You're half an hour early.'

'Yeah, well.'

'No problem. We should meet.'

'Where?'

'I'll pick you up in twenty minutes.'

'Great. Terrific.'

'Bye.'

'Bye.'

A black hole, an airless, dustless, thoughtless vacuum of nothing. Nineteen minutes to go. It briefly occurred to Drew that this was ruining his vacation.

The car was a brick-brown Honda. Peter got out as Drew walked up.

'Hey,' Peter greeted.

'Hi,' Drew said, 'glad you came.'

'Uh, listen,' Peter said, 'I brought a few friends along. Hope you don't mind.'

Getting in the car, 'Drew, this is Dan and Arthur. Guys, this is my friend Drew from America.'

Drew locked eyes with Peter. Peter raised his eyebrows, and the car sped off into Sydney traffic.

Well.

At dinner:

'So,' Dan asked, 'how long have you two Yanks known each other?'

Drew had no response to this.

'Since we were kids,' Peter said. 'Our parents were mutual friends.'

He glanced over to Drew, forcibly passing the baton. Hand it back? or . . .

'The age difference was a little much for us to be really close, but our families kept kind of intertwining,' Drew sighed complicitly.

Peter didn't smile or offer any overt thanks, but his body settled in a satisfied way.

'So when I was planning my trip, I thought I'd look Peter up.'

'Well, that's great,' said Arthur. 'It's always nice to have friends overseas.'

'Yeah,' Dan continued, 'we've got a friend in Germany we always stay with when we go . . .'

And off they all went to Europe, and the tapestry for the evening began to be woven, until it got thick enough to smother. The rest of the dinner conversation was the same charade with only one noteworthy exchange. Arthur was speaking: 'And then out of the record store walks Nathan, this guy Peter used to date, and he . . .' Drew looked across at Peter. Peter smiled and shrugged. Drew sighed. *Uncle*, he thought and surrendered.

Drew looked back over the years and it seemed absurdly impossible that he could have missed it. Missing Dan and Arthur was one thing, his mind had been on other things entirely. But not once in the admittedly staccato times that Drew and Peter had spent together had Drew sensed anything. At all. Peter hadn't even mentioned it at lunch, even after he had pretty much nailed Drew's own private truths to his forehead. Maybe it was because Drew had never expected it, had never gone looking.

What's going on? Drew thought. *Have I lost every one of my bearings?*

Loud. And loud. And loud. They had gone to a club.
  'What?!'

'What did you say!?'

'This is hopeless!'

It was all crash, clamor and silence.

And then of course it was late. And of course Peter was tired. And of course the evening was over. The drive to Drew's hotel passed in the same silence that had muffled the past two hours. Drew accepted that he'd been defeated and tried to be gracious. As they approached, he said, 'I've got another day here in Sydney, want to try to get together tomorrow?'

Peter made a half-wince of apology. Drew was surprised when he said, 'Yeah, sure.' There was a contradiction there somewhere.

'I'll call you in the morning,' Peter said.

'Oh,' Drew said, getting out of the car.

'I will,' Peter insisted, but only slightly. 'We'll go to the beach. Or something.'

Drew smiled to mask the importance of this to Dan and Arthur. 'Nice meeting you both; it was fun.' And to Peter: 'If I don't hear from you by ten, you'll know I'll have given up.'

He shut the car door, turned, and went into the hotel, shellshocked.

What happened just there?

IV

Up by six. Showered and groomed by six-thirty. Body clenched tight as a fist by 6:45. The jetlag had dwindled to the point of making Drew simply an early-rising Sydneysider. He breakfasted at the hotel café after explaining in quite annoying detail just how important it was for him to be retrieved if anyone called. He forced his way through his coffee, purposely black, and therefore undrinkable, to encourage deliberation. After nearly two hours, he looked at his watch. It was 7:25. *Fucking hell*, he thought.

His overwhelming impression of the previous night was of sudden entropy. As if, after blithely running through dandelion seeds, he had suddenly found himself immersed in salt, only able to move millimeters although not really at all. If you know what he means. Drew is clearly becoming useless to us again but fortunately, there is a phone call:

'It's Mom,' smiled the hotel counter girl who, up until now, had seemed so kind.

For a moment, Drew considered excuses. (*Tell her I'm out. Tell her I'm sleeping. Tell her I hate her, for Christ's sake.*) Then Malevolent Counter Girl said into the receiver, 'He's right here.' She offered the phone to Drew.

Deep breath. Another. Swallow.

'Mom?'

'Hi, son! How's it going? Are you having a good time?'

'Hi, mom.'

'How's the weather? We got your postcard! Can't believe it got here so fast!'

'Six days isn't long plus remember –'

'Yes, the dateline, I know. Isn't that just the weirdest thing?'

'Um . . .'

'Did you get to the opera like you planned?'

'Yeah, *Don Giovanni*.'

'Means nothing to me. Is the opera house as neat as it looks on TV?'

Drew saw the girl pick up Line 2 out of the corner of his eye.

'Mom . . .'

'Your father's in the hospital again.'

('Powell Sydney Hotel, can I help you?')

'What?'

('Actually, he's standing right here on another line. Isn't that funny? Can I take a message and have him call you?')

'His toe again. He'll be okay, but it's sure got him down.'

('Six o'clock. Sure.')

'Look, Mom, I've . . .,' frantically waving his hands.

('I'll give him the message.')

'Yeah, I know, this is costing me a fortune. Call us when you get back.'

('Bye.')

'Bye, Mom.' He hung up before he heard her reply. 'Wait!' He lunged at the girl as she hung up the phone.

'Shit!' he said, too loudly. Heads turned in the lobby.

'Oh, sorry,' she smiled at him, oblivious to all despair inflicted. 'Well, he seemed in quite a hurry anyway. Here's the message. He'll pick you up at six, something's come up.'

Drew took the message. It said, *Peter says he'll pick you up at six, something's come up.*

'Pick me up here?' Drew asked.

'Presumably,' she said with enough good cheer to blind. Drew looked at his watch. Ten hours, twenty-two minutes to go. He grabbed his hair with both hands.

'Oh, man,' he said.

And there it sat. The day. Having made no real itinerary from the beginning, he was faced with the common mistake of novices on vacation: nothing to do. His only formulated plan from a few days ago was 'the beach or something, it's Australia for Christ's sake, someone will come up and offer me things.'

Instead, he walked.

There was a sort of path, not more than an undeveloped block really, near where Drew lived as a child called the Cherry Tree Trail. A purely functional title; simple, nothing haunted. Drew wouldn't have known a cherry tree from a telephone pole, so he had no idea of the accuracy of the name, but it was a place to go on those rare occasions when enough children in the neighborhood coalesced to do something as a group. If pressed, Drew could only have actually recalled a single time that this happened, but whole childhoods are built around less. It suffices.

This is the memory: No common enemy, no bully from which to hide, and no common goal either, no hunt. Just four or five (or seven or eight) children slowly moving through waxy underbrush and the thick wholesome dirt smell of towering conifers that successfully blotted out signs of suburbia. There is an attention-needer in the group, as always, but he is satisfied by an audience of only two, leaving the others to keep to their own conversations (so there must be more than four, but certainly not more than ten or one group would become two). Weaving under and over tree branches, not everyone always speaks to everyone else but no one leaves the gravitational pull of the group. There is no point to the group, really, except to exist together like water molecules pulled into a drop. The key here is not individuality, because in the burn-and-rest lives of the very young, the different one always remains the different *one*. After a time, the group bivouacs, and whole bolts of nothing occur. Then splinters of two and the quick wait for sunset. Then each goes home alone, whittled down into exhaustion.

Drew could only remember the names of two friends from this far back in childhood: Angela, whose father was black and mother was white, and Jeremy, who lived in an A-frame house that, if nothing else, was singular. Drew turned around. He half-expected to see one of them getting out of a cab. There was only a man and his young son playing chess on a park bench.

Where was he? The Royal Botanical Gardens again. It was a crisp October spring day, pulled taut by its own length. The sky was a gorgeous asphyxiated-child blue with some saliva foam clouds spat here and there. It was like a really bright and lovely funeral. Drew could have cried. Odd. He hadn't cried at his brother's funeral. Looking back on it again, Drew could see the closed coffin, a (pseudo-, it's turned out) military-issue dark brown, some flowers, a few relatives, scads of just people who felt they should show up. And all the while Drew sitting, itching, craving, *dying* to leave, to get out, to flee. So now he finally had, only his brother had beaten him to it.

There it was. Well, goddamn it, there it was.

'Hold on a minute, let me check.'

A pause.

'There's no answer in his room. Can I take a message?'

'Yeah, tell him Peter called, and I'm sorry but I won't be able to make it.'

'All righty.'

She wrote the message and scrawled 314 at its top. The other girl behind the counter watched her put it in the message box.

'314?' the second girl said.

'Yeh.'

'The American fellow?'

'Yeh?'

'He checked out half an hour ago. You were at lunch.'

'Really? But he was real keen on seeing this Peter fellow earlier.'

'Guess he isn't now. He took a cab to the airport. Then it's off to Alice, I think he said.'

'Hm.' She crumpled the note and tossed it in the garbage.

And we race through them because, although lovely, they're nothing exceptional (well, to anyone but Drew) . . .

Alice Springs and Uluru were heat-blasted, blinding,

and thrumming with purpose. At sunrise, it really and truly did change colors. Cairns was lots of rowdy, touristy fun: kangaroos, wallabies, koalas, and wombats; a Great Barrier Reef dive off a sailboat chartered especially for a group of homos; a chance for another smiling indiscretion. Then to Brisbane for the international flight and a seat next to a young Australian man who would not stop bouncing.

'First time out of Australia,' he said without prompting, rubbing his hands on his pant legs.

'Oh, really?' Drew said, feeling genuinely good. 'How exciting. Just a holiday?'

'Yeh, off on an adventure, I guess.' He lowered his voice to a conspiratorial level, 'I'm so excited, I'm about to piss my pants.' He snorted, embarrassed, and bounced some more unconsciously.

'Just out of college?' Drew asked.

'Yup, just done, well, not quite done. Didn't actually finish. Didn't really actually start. Not really. Wasn't real good at it, you know? At uni? Trip's a present from my folks. Reckon they think I'll get my head in line or find myself or something.'

He laughed again.

'And what would you do if you found yourself?' Drew asked.

'Dunno,' he said, and stopped moving for the first time. He smiled again. 'Buy myself a beer, maybe? Kick my ass for being such a layabout?'

They laughed easily, warmly.

'You?' the young man asked back.

'If I found myself?'

'Yeh.'

Drew exhaled through his nose and considered. The plane roared forward and upward. Away and away and away.

2,115 opportunities

Reality 1, 22 July, 12:48–53pm

The 'first' time, Ryan (Subject 1) sits alone at the booth, nodding his head absently to The Ramones on the jukebox (some joker has inexplicably selected 'Pet Sematary' over a live 'I Wanna Be Sedated' from the CD offerings), looking through the window to the outdoor tables on the other side, angling his view just so in order to appear not to be staring at four rich-looking teenagers (dusted leather sandals, gold necklaces out-expensing ugly) sharing an afternoon bite with a dog (labrador, chocolate), no doubt on their way to or from the beach during the current summer break, sitting out in the sunny afternoon under a blue sky that looks badly in need of a wipe with a damp cloth.

Ryan is through the black coffee he's ordered and is awaiting a refill before finishing off the diner's eponymous burger with bacon and, for exoticism's sake, a slice of provolone cheese. He is a motorcycle messenger on his lunch break, spending a little more than usual for a sit-down lunch for no other reason than another plain-wrapped-flour-tortilla with assorted-vegetables-and-chicken-bits eaten while standing seems a failure of justice after five straight hours of trips to and from a single, indecisive company with offices in Venice and downtown. In any other city, he'd be a plain bike messenger, but Los Angeles, for good and ill, isn't any other city. It is a place where a mere bicycle is no good to anybody.

Ryan has recently broken up with his girlfriend (Clare, Sagittarius) after she discovered an occasion of infidelity on his part with a secretary from a delivery destination. Said liaison lasted a single night but left behind enough evidence (smear of non-Clare-coloured lipstick on an off-white sheet) to send Clare packing. Ryan tries not to mind, especially seeing how the pertinent liaison was merely one among a larger undiscovered number of infidelities that Ryan saw himself the victim of, but he had been fumbling towards loving Clare, loving her full behind and dyed-goth hair, loving her leather knee boots, her spangly wrists and even her permanently-in-estrus Siamese, Poo-Tee-Tweet. Such sentiments, offered authentically if inarticulately, were not enough to keep Clare from removing her toothbrush from Ryan's bathroom.

The waitress (in vintage waitress miniskirt and ironic fishnets) refills Ryan's coffee, and Ryan re-commences the burger, dripping burger juice onto one thigh and rubbing it absently off the padded leather that is the uniform of the motorcycle messenger. He glances at his watch and requests the check. It is $8.75. He leaves a crumpled ten-dollar bill with 'Jamie' written on it in blue ballpoint, grabs his helmet and leaves the diner as that Split Enz song about a leaky boat begins to play on the jukebox.

Seven minutes later, Magda (Subject 2) enters the café.

Realities 2–84, 22 July, 12:34–55pm (various)
As above with the vagaries of Southland traffic altering the duration of Ryan's lunch and the difference between

his exit from the diner and Magda's entrance from a maximum of thirteen minutes but never less than a minimum of five minutes.

Reality 85, 22 July, 12:47–58pm
Ryan decides to buy a newspaper to read at lunch, reducing the time difference between himself and Magda to ninety seconds.

Realities 86–207, 22 July, 12:33–59pm (various)
As above with the vagaries of Southland traffic altering the duration of Ryan's lunch and newspaper-reading and the difference between Ryan's exit from the diner and Magda's entrance from a maximum of seven minutes but never less than a minimum of 28 seconds.

Aberrant Realities 89 & 171, 22 July, 12:01pm & 11:58am (respectively)
Twice, the clutch on Ryan's motorcycle sticks while on the 10 Freeway; on one occasion (89) forcing him to call the Auto Club and therefore never reaching the diner. On the second occasion (171) Ryan loses control of the motorcycle and skids into a guardrail, cracking his helmet and nearly decapitating himself. He is mourned by a Polish-immigrant mother and a mascara-streaked Clare. Both Realities removed from sample.

Reality 208, 22 July, 12:56–1:00pm

Magda (Subject 2), an intelligent girl and therefore punished by society, is vastly underemployed as a book-keeper for various small businesses up and down Beverly Boulevard. She wears her hair in a short bob that swoops forward to tightly bracket her face, and she usually dresses in mostly black with pale pancake make-up. It is a full-body mask she wears to keep at arm's length her (mostly friendly) employers: the laundrymen of various exotic ethnicities, the Honduran florist, the Algerians who own the vegetarian restaurant. She started dressing as a goth (with the occasional Stevie Nicks influence) at 14, felt comfortable behind it, and never saw any reason to change as she grew older.

On a Thursday (today), she looks through the weekly accounts of an arty video and DVD rental store (called 24 Times Per Second, an expensive trademark that Magda has successfully disguised as a legitimate-looking business expense). Magda leans more than slightly towards Obsessive-Compulsive Disorder, a trait which has made her, at 25, a stunningly capable book-keeper, but which has also segregated her day into rigid sections. Every Thursday, she finishes 24 Times' books at exactly 12:58pm, allowing her a two-minute walk to the diner down the street (a self-consciously retro and hip representation of the fifties mixed with an updated punk feel that in itself is probably ten years past). She arrives at the diner at 1:00pm exactly, sits in the same booth, reads whatever paperback she's selected from her to-be-read shelf (currently *Lolita*, formerly *Girl in Landscape*, soon to be *The Man in the High Castle*), and orders the same large chicken Caesar salad. She is aware that she does this as a ritual, but she does not feel compelled as yet to address it as a problem.

It is only by a mistake that begins in this Reality (208) that she arrives at the diner one minute and 22 seconds early. The source of this mistake is this morning when, during her daily habit of setting her watch to the ticker running across the bottom of the news network she has on in the background behind her regimented breakfast (frosted cornflakes, two pieces of buttered white toast, a 'tropical' blend of fruit juices and sugar), she is unaware (as how could she possibly not be?) that the computer news ticker has suffered a brief power surge during the night and that a lazy intern has re-set the ticker to his own (fast by one minute and 22 seconds) watch rather than the Greenwich Mean Time clock meant to keep the entire international news team synchronised. The error is corrected while Magda is at work, but of course, this is too late for Magda.

Today (Thursday, 208, *ibid*), Magda arrives at the diner 82 seconds earlier than in Realities 1–207. Ryan, newspaper tucked under one arm, helmet in hand, brushes past her as they come through opposite sides of the entrance to the diner. He turns as she moves past him. She doesn't acknowledge him, but he recognises her. He opens his mouth to speak but realises he cannot remember her name or where he knows her from. He watches as she moves to her regular table and orders her regular dish.

He shrugs and walks to his motorcycle.

Realities 209–755, 22 July, 12:56–59pm

This Reality repeats itself an unusually high number of times with only negligible variation (the amount of powder on Magda's face, the phrasing of a punchline in a single comic in Ryan's newspaper ('Look, I can't see what's so hard about this' becomes 'Look, I don't see what's so hard about this' and stays that way)).

Aberrant Realities 311, 417 & 685, 22 July, 12:58pm, 9:21am & unknown (respectively)

In 311, Magda is the victim of a gunshot wound when 24 Times Per Second is mistaken for an amphetamine lab by an over-eager police recruit who has mixed up his addresses. She survives but obviously does not make it to the diner. In 417, a left-on deep-fat fryer finally ignites after an entire night of simmering, burning the diner and the adjacent hotel to the ground in under ninety minutes. Ryan eats at McDonald's. An upset Magda returns home and doesn't leave the house again that day. In 685, an evolutionary disaster has disallowed the existence of all life forms larger than microbial. All Realities removed from sample.

Reality 756, 22 July, 12:59–1:01pm

Ryan watches as she moves to her regular table and orders her regular dish. He shrugs and walks to his motorcycle. As he is pulling away, recognition dawns and he says, 'Magda,' to the inside of his helmet.

Realities 757–1,310, 22 July, 12:59–1:01pm (various)

Recognition for Subject 1 arrives at various intervals for 553 realities as the sugar and caffeine levels in his brain and bloodstream move up and down due to slight variances in diet from the previous night through to the morning. For each of these 553 Realities, Subject 1's recognition of Subject 2 as someone he knows comes too late in the process of walking to his motorcycle for him to try and catch her attention. And then, it doesn't.

Reality 1,311, 22 July, 12:51–58pm

The one thousand, three hundred and eleventh time, Ryan (Subject 1) sits alone at the booth, nodding his head absently to Peter Gabriel on the jukebox (someone has chosen 'Games Without Frontiers' from the CD offerings), looking through the window to the outdoor tables on the other side, angling his view just so in order to appear not to be staring at four rich-looking Hispanic teenagers (pleated khaki trousers, woven leather sandals) out for an afternoon bite with a dog (pit bull, mottled), no doubt on their way to or from the beach during the current summer break, sitting out under a blue sky spattered with dribbled clouds.

Ryan is through the vanilla shake he's ordered and is awaiting a glass of water before finishing off the café's crispy club sandwich. The waitress (in an ironic but sexy re-interpretation of a mechanic's jumpsuit) brings Ryan's water, and Ryan re-commences the sandwich, idly flipping another page of the sports section (he perversely

163

supports the ne'er-do-well basketball team of the city's two and is pleased beyond words to read that they've beaten their over-paid, over-arrogant, over-featured municipal rival). He glances at his watch and requests the check. It is $9.25. Ryan leaves a crumpled ten-dollar bill with '8/7/1992' written on it in blue ballpoint along with a few coins, grabs his helmet and leaves his seat as 'Message to my Girl' comes over the jukebox.

Magda, meanwhile, is walking from her bookkeeping job at Flicker Fusion (a video and DVD rental store that Magda secretly feels is too up its own cinephile ass for its own good) down Beverly Boulevard to the diner where she always eats on a Thursday (also slightly up its own ass but with decent food and unspeakably good poppyseed cake). Her shoulder-length hair swoops down over her face as she stares at the sidewalk, ignoring the sun as much with her glance as she has with her wardrobe. She holds *The Verificationist* under one arm to read over lunch, though it is a short book and she has a copy of *The Names* in her purse should she finish before the hour is over.

She is two minutes and one second early in all of her dealings with the day due to computer error on the ticker of the financial network by which she sets her watch each morning. The error is fixed while Magda is at work, but Magda, of course, does not know this. It would upset her to a degree that would embarrass her if she found out, and it is lucky for the purposes of this sample that she does not.

Today (Thursday, 1,311, *ibid*), Magda arrives at the diner 121 seconds earlier than she normally does. Ryan, newspaper tucked under one arm, helmet in hand, looks up as he opens the door to leave. He turns as she moves past.

'Magda?' he says.

She stops, curious, slightly annoyed that her lunch is being interrupted. She arches an eyebrow as a shield. She cocks her head.

'Brian, isn't it?'

Reality 1,311 (continued), 2 May, 11:31pm

They have met before but only very briefly, introduced fleetingly by friends of friends of friends at a party. She catches his eye because she is carrying a beer bottle in one hand and a book in the other (remarkably enough, *The Recognitions* by William Gaddis, all 954 pages of it).

'Who brings a book to a party?'

It is the wrong thing to say, and he knows it as soon as it leaves his lips, as soon as it reaches her face.

'I do, obviously.'

He is slightly drunk, so he is unable to muster a response as he watches her walk away.

Realities 1,312–1,407, 22 July, 12:58–59pm (various)

As Reality 1,311 with negligible variation.

Aberrant Reality 1,348, 22 July, 12:59pm

In Reality 1,348, Subject 2 is a lesbian. Though she and

Subject 1 end up at the diner at the same time, they take no notice of each other whatsoever. Reality removed from sample.

Reality 1,408, 22 July, 12:59–1:11pm
'Ryan, isn't it?'

'You remembered.'

'So did you.'

'Yes.'

'So. How's it going?' This said with slight hostility, as Magda is eager to carry on with her pre-planned meal.

'Good, good, good. Just had some lunch.'

'Fancy that, coming out of a diner at lunchtime. Who'd a thought?'

'Okay. Catch you later then, all right?'

'Yeah, maybe.'

As he carries on out into the sunshine, Magda frowns to herself. She feels she has been rude but can't quite remember why she should have been to this boy with the ring in his eyebrow. She assumes that it's because her lunch has now been delayed by precious seconds and chides herself for once again being such a slave to her internal regime.

She is still in a state of mild fret when her entrée arrives.

Realities 1,409–1,633, 22 July, 12:58–1:01pm (various)
Over the course of these 224 Realities, Subject 2 displays

a nimble mind and seems especially responsive to variations in reality stimuli (certainly more than Subject 1). Subject 2's Obsessive-Compulsive Disorder (undiagnosed) should be noted. Following are samples taken at random from the above subsection.

Sample Reality 1,417, 22 July, 12:59–1:01pm
'Ryan, isn't it?'
  'You remembered.'
'I did, yes.'
'Yes.'
'So. How's it going?'
'Good, good, good. Just had some lunch.'
'Fancy that, coming out of a diner at lunchtime.'
'Okay. Catch you later then, all right?'
'All right.'

Sample Reality 1,491, 22 July, 12:59–1:01pm
'Ryan, isn't it?'
  'You remembered.'
'That party at Adam's.'
'Yeah.'
'So. How's it going?'
'Good, good, good. Just had some lunch.'
'Who'd have guessed?' (But the intonation has lowered its sarcasm and raised a (slightly) friendly tease.)
  'Okay. Catch you later then, all right?'
  'Yeah, okay.'

Sample Reality 1,576, 22 July, 12:59–1:01pm

'Ryan, isn't it?'

'You remembered.'

'That party at Adam's.'

'Oh, yeah.'

'How's it going then?'

'Good, good, good. Just had some lunch.'

'Who'd have guessed?' (And this time an actual smile.)

'Guess so, yeah.' Ryan smiles in return. 'Catch you later then, all right?'

'Yeah, okay.'

Reality 1,634, 22 July, 12:59–1:12pm

And then Subject 2 elaborates.

'It's Ryan, isn't it?'

'You remembered.'

'You were at that party at Adam's.'

'Oh, yeah.'

'And you made fun of me for carrying a book.'

Ryan glances at the book she currently has under one arm (*Mao II*) but says nothing.

'Did I?'

'You did.'

'God, I'm sorry. I must have been drunk.'

'Must have been. Look, I'm kind of in a hurry . . .'

'Okay. Catch you later then, all right?'

'Yeah, okay.'

As he carries on out into the sunshine, Magda frowns to herself. She has been rude but she is wondering whether it was correct to do so. She assumes her irritation is most likely because her lunch has now been delayed by precious seconds and chides herself for once again being such a slave to her internal regime.

She is still in a state of mild fret when her entrée arrives.

Realities 1,635–2,113, 22 July, 12:58–1:14pm (various)

The ensuing 478 Realities display a similar loop as the cycle of Realities 1,409–1,633, when the following occurs:

As Ryan carries on out into the sunshine, Magda frowns to herself. She has been rude but wonders whether it was correct to do so. She assumes at first that her irritation is most likely because her lunch has now been delayed by precious seconds and chides herself for once again being such a slave to her internal regime.

She is still in a state of mild fret when her entrée arrives. Before even taking a bite of her Salad Nicoise, she decides that she was in fact rude to Ryan and makes a mental note to apologise to him should she ever run into him again.

Reality 2,114, 22 July, 12:51–1:05pm

The two thousand, one hundred and fourteenth time, Ryan (Subject 1) sits alone at the booth, nodding his head absently to XTC on the jukebox ('Senses Working Overtime'), looking through the window to the outdoor tables on the other side, angling his view just so in order to appear not to be staring at the Hispanic teenagers (ratty blue jeans, cut off tees, all with mobile phones) out for an afternoon bite with a dog (blue-grey mongrel), no doubt on their way from the beach during the current summer break, sitting out under a blue sky towering with cumulonimbus clouds approaching from off the ocean, clouds that will threaten and threaten but never quite rain.

Ryan is through the black coffee he's ordered and is awaiting a refill before finishing off the café's epony-mous burger with bacon and, for exoticism's sake, a slice of gorgonzola cheese. The waitress (in a vintage mini-skirt but wearing plastic red devil horns) brings Ryan's refill, and Ryan re-commences his meal, dripping burger juice onto the sports section of the newspaper he is reading. He glances at his watch and requests the check. It is $8.50. Ryan leaves a crumpled ten dollar bill with 'Cumbria' written on it in blue ballpoint, grabs his helmet and leaves his seat as a Finn Brothers track he doesn't recognize comes on the jukebox.

Magda, meanwhile, is walking from her book-keeping job at Chiaroscuro (a video and DVD rental store) down Beverly Boulevard to the diner where she always eats on a Thursday (slightly too fond of itself but with decent food and peculiarly excellent iced tea). Her bobbed, dyed-red hair swoops down over her face as she stares at the sidewalk, ignoring the sun as much with her glance as she has with her wardrobe. She holds *The Sot-Weed Factor* under one arm to read over lunch.

She is two minutes and eleven seconds early in all of her dealings with the day due to a computer error on the ticker of the local morning news by which she sets her watch each morning. The error is not fixed for nearly a week, and Magda is not the only city-dweller who is slightly early for the next seven days.

Today, Magda arrives at the diner 131 seconds earlier than normal. Ryan, newspaper tucked under one arm, helmet in hand, looks up at her as he opens the door to leave. He turns as she moves past him.

'Magda?' he says.

She stops, curious, slightly annoyed that her lunch is being interrupted. She arches an eyebrow as a shield. She cocks her head.

'It's Ryan, isn't it?'

'You remembered.'

'You were at that party at Adam's.'

'Oh, yeah.'

'And you made fun of me for carrying a book.'

Ryan glances at the book she currently has under one arm but says nothing.

'I did, didn't I? Sorry, I was kind of stupid drunk that night.'

'That's all right.'

'I mean, I read, too.'

Magda holds up the book to show him. 'Read this?'

'No, but I've read *Giles Goat-Boy*.'

Magda is surprised. 'Really?'

'Yeah, really.'

Magda curls her lip in a way that strikes Ryan as attractive. He looks at his watch, but only as an affectation because he doesn't even register the current time (1:01pm).

'Look,' he says, 'I've got a little bit of time left. Mind if I join you?'

'Haven't you already eaten?'

'I'll just have a coffee. We can chat.'

Something (perhaps the handsome mess of his hair, ruffled by his helmet: perhaps the scar on his upper lip that makes his smile cutely crooked: perhaps she is just feeling lonely this afternoon) makes Magda pause and act contrary to her natural behavior.

'Yeah, sure,' she says. 'Why not?'

Reality 2,115, 22 July, 1:00pm
Neither Subject 1 nor Subject 2 eat at the diner that day, because:

Reality 2,115 (continued), 2 May, 11:32pm
'Do you mind if I ask why you brought a book to a party?' His smile is a friendly one, almost familiar. She doesn't take offense. She shows him the book (*The Atrocity Exhibition*).

'In case I didn't meet anyone.'

'Well, you've met someone now.'

Approximately two and a half months later, on 22 July, as has become their Thursday ritual, Subject 1 brings Chinese takeaway to Subject 2's place of work (a DVD and video rental store called Ton Et Lumiere). They talk quietly and privately among themselves, laughing under an umbrella, eating their wontons as the rain sprinkles down.

the motivations of
Sally Rae Wentworth, Amazon

Lucia 'Tippi' Ponce-Jones takes Julian Buxton, starts war

The truce, which had become pretty rusty as the years ticked by anyway, was finally broken for good and all when Lucia 'Tippi' Ponce-Jones, administrative assistant to the Amazonian Vice Priestess of Reading & Bracknell (Inclusive), smote Hemel Palethorpe Gull & Gull Chartered Accountant Julian Buxton on the back of the head with a redwood birthing board at the Hemel Palethorpe Gull & Gull annual summer picnic and rounders game, knocking him unconscious and dragging him by his already thinning hair to her one-bedroom hut just off the M4 near Slough, impressing him into lifelong concubinage. Because the picnic/rounders game was being held miles away from Slough on Camberwell Green and therefore well inside the generally agreed Central London Non-Hostility Zone – having been relocated from Hampstead, where an outbreak of malaria had felled most of the Highgate Ursuline Sisters of Mercy Charity Football Summer League and where also the crocs in the men's bathing pond had shown higher aggression of late, consuming at least three swimmers as well as a bushwalker with no doubt lecherous intent; and because such a kidnapping was a direct violation of Clause 5, Section 4, of the Non-Hostilities Pact 1985 in any event, regardless of area; and because Ponce-Jones, though not *in* the Amazonian governmental hierarchy herself per se, *was* nevertheless in line for a title and therefore directly affiliated with the Amazonian government, being, as mentioned, the administrative assistant to Vice Priestess Margaret Hassellbeck; and finally because Buxton, aside from being a fully qualified Chartered Accountant and therefore off-limits regardless, was also Deputy Treasurer for the Protectorate National Society of Chartered Accountants, Southern Division, and therefore an actual junior member of the Chartered Accountancy Government; for all reasons stated above, all-out war was more or less inevitable.

Which complicated my life to no end.

You may have heard of me

I, being your narrator, am named Sally Rae Thomasina Wentworth, Sally Rae being my two-name first name after my mother Sally RaeAnne Chenowith, of the Charleston, South Carolina Chenowiths, and Thomasina being after my father, Thomas Quiller Wentworth of the Atlanta, Georgia Wentworths. I was born forty-seven years ago in Savannah, Georgia, in the United Protestant States of America to Mr and Mrs Wentworth before they took up their permanent commission as missionaries for the American Southern Baptist Church of Christ In God to the Amazon Nation of Great Britain when I was the age of ten years. This first, and last, posting for Mr and Mrs Wentworth (young narrator in tow) was the Isle of Man.

I am from the American South, but I am not of it,

whereas I am *of* the Isle of Man but not *from* it. This is important.

It is possible, depending upon your personal, individual attentions, that you may have heard of me or may at least have seen me on television standing next to or near or in the vicinity of Queen Joanne II on state or diplomatic occasions. I serve HRH in the capacity of Domestic Affairs Advisor, an appointed position rather than one selected from the House of Commons, as my place of birth, being no fault of my own, nevertheless prevents me from serving in HRH's Parliament as an elected official. This is both important and not. I am a member of HRH's cabinet but am destined to remain forever *ex officio*.

This is not a complaint. I am honoured to serve HRH, long may she reign.

War begins with an attack on the Chartered Accountancy Protectorate Luton Arms Depot, and also with paperwork

Although the definitive action that brought on the war – Ponce-Jones' impressment of Buxton – was taken by an Amazon, HRH, in a typical display of initiative and with the aid of advice proffered by your narrator, decided to attack the Chartered Accountancy Protectorate first, because if war was inevitable, why not 'act boldly in the best Amazonian tradition' (said HRH, parroting me) and just get the whole thing started off to the best advantage of our side? Makes sense.

Two squadrons of forty soldiers attacked the CAP Arms Depot near Luton. Leaving their horses behind so as to blitz in the silence that only highly trained troops of the Amazonian army can muster, the eighty soldiers plus four sergeants plus one captain set on the surprisingly under-defended depot, taking it quickly and with minimal loss of life on our side. Fifteen CAP soldiers were killed: the remaining six were impressed. The first casualties of war. ('Twenty-one soldiers to guard an important arms depot?' asked HRH, quite rightly. 'Why did we wait so long to attack them, is my question.') Only two Amazons were killed, two more welcome guests at the Great Feast, lucky sows.

A lot of paperwork was involved as well, and fortunately I have competent and capable assistants to handle most of it or I would be buried because war generates forms and reports like nothing else on Goddess' Green Earth. When, for illustrative purposes, HRH launched an initiative against the French Farmer's Republic Isle of Jersey when I was the newly appointed Deputy Assistant Domestic Affairs Advisor, under the late Dame Edith Chalwin-Prichard, it took seventeen different personnel in our office alone not excluding myself nor Dame Edith (about whom let it never be said that she was afraid of real grunt work) to type the necessary documentation. And that was for a wee little island with nothing on it but an amusement park that HRH had taken a fancy to, which of course didn't stop the FFR from causing a ridiculously overblown kerfuffle in the Assembly of Nations, as if that feeble bunch of do-nothings ever once accomplished anything useful or indeed at all.

But from the CAP Depot, yes. Mountains of paper-work but nearly 600 spears and over 400 muskets were taken, and I ask you, if the CAP were not anticipating war, despite their repeated claims, why would they have such a fully stocked depot? I ask you.

Naturalization

As you will have gathered from the brief history above (of which more in a moment) I am a naturalized Amazon, having completed citizenship proceedings at the age of twenty-one with six hundred and eleven other hopefuls in a very moving ceremony hosted by HRH herself. We held our hands across our chests, bodies sheathed in formal leather singlets, a ceremonial bow or spear or flail as per personal preference in our free hand, and renounced all ties to inferior pasts, becoming by procla-mation Amazons, despite a noticeable lack of height in comparison to the sternly helpful Immigration Officers present and the sternly kind personage of HRH, looming down at us with the one and only real Sceptre of War in one hand and the actual immensely impressive Mace of Might in the other, thereby underlining for all six hundred and twelve freshly minted Amazons the real and true sombreness and seriousness and underlying importance of the ceremony we had just gone through.

For me, for one, it was the least they could do.

The motivations of Lucia 'Tippi' Ponce-Jones

Why, in a question that gets lost in the mists of time – or the rasping, raking, grabbing claws of time or the general vague yet unshakeable depressing fog of time, your choice – did Lucia 'Tippi' Ponce-Jones so boldly break a years and years-old truce for the sake of the individual man Julian Buxton? Or more succinctly, why do wars begin?

I have talked myself into a corner there, do you see? I know the answer to the first question, but I do not, in fact, know any such answer to the second. Why *do* wars begin? Any wars at all. You may be surprised to hear this from me yet nevertheless I am here to tell you that nothing good ever comes from any war. Ever. Of any kind. Only scarred and scared generations of young dying on front lines, puffing up only those old and powerful and arrogant and, most importantly, distant enough to imagine themselves as the hand of destiny, the God or Goddess of War (for the Amazons to whom I have allieged are far from guiltless), directing the fates of worlds when it's really only the fates of the twenty-somethings and, heaven save us from our sins, teenagers who we send to die and die and die. Notice how it's always called the 'spoils' of war. Medals of coagulated blood, celebration pyres for the dead, telegrams and letters and emails now of grief in terse sentences. At least Amazons are guaranteed seats at the Great Feast if they die in battle.

If you believe that. Which sometimes, if I'm honest with you, I wonder, especially now that 'battle' has expanded the definition of itself to include such things as death by natural causes after retirement from being a shopping-centre security guard or death by car crash if the dogcatcher wagon overturns, watering down I think the Great Feast table into just another boring convention of uniformed women. I wonder.

But, yes, again the motivations of Lucia 'Tippi' Ponce-Jones. It was love clearly or at least what the young so often mistake for love and, frankly, who are we in middle age to say that it *isn't* love, that rush of adrenalin and hormones that feels hot and cool at the same time like a frozen creamy cocktail. Why is that not love but yes this companionable settling that we do as life goes on is? Maybe love really is only for the young and the old co-opt it as we do everything and call our watered-down if quite comfortable version the only 'real' love. Tippi was in love with Julian Buxton. I could see it with my own two eyes. Simple. Plain as the nose on your face. Because if the fizz in her voice and behind her smile and in the flush of her skin wasn't love, then why bother with love at all and not just take whatever it is she has? If Tippi wasn't in love, then love's been scooped by something that looks far better or at least more fun, is my opinion.

The missionary work of the ASBCofCinG on the Isle of Man

My parents Mr and Mrs Wentworth were young, too, when they arrived on the Isle of Man with ten-year-old me along as something they could cling to. They were both twenty-six years old. Twenty-six. Can you imagine a twenty-six-year-old these days moving across the ocean with spouse and child in tow for no salary, only living expenses, suffering deprivations including no running water for the first year, all to preach an evangelist gospel of mostly American nonsense but with a few good ideas interspersed including pacifism which was like kerosene on a campfire as far as the Amazons were concerned? Nor can I, though I suppose they must exist because as far as I know the ASBCofCinG Missionary Service is still around, sending off dazed smiling youths (maybe) filled with the fire of God or at least a challenge or at the very least ham-fisted good intentions, off to parts unknown, unexplored, unChristianised certainly, sending them to serious hardship, certain struggle, potential doom. I wonder what those missionaries look like now, though I wouldn't want to meet one to find out, I don't think.

My parents were true believers which 37 years ago was less of a thing. Earnest and fresh-faced and eager to proselytise, they moved into a tiny central terraced house in Jurby East. Why not Douglas? Why not Castletown or even Peel? I do not know. Jurby East was where the church sent them and Jurby East is where they went. Isolated amongst Amazons, miles from the nearest town, they set to work. They started operating a little church in our sitting-room, and for a very long time, my mother and father took turns making up half of the congregation of two while the other preached to me and whoever's turn it was.

My parents, in a ludicrous oversight all too common amongst purveyors of do-goodery, had not been taught to speak Amazonian. They were expected to pick up the language from the Manx Amazons. Being a child language-sponge, this meant practically that *I* at ten years of age was expected to learn the language and translate for them. As I was not, however, allowed by Amazonian law to attend an Amazonian school, this was problematic. Nor were we permitted to shop in any Amazonian store save a piss-poor designated one six miles away, nor could we attend Amazonian movies, nor own a car to drive on Amazonian roads, nor bank in any Amazonian savings institution, and on and on. To say that missionaries were barely tolerated by the Amazonian government is to risk over-generosity. They didn't want my parents there but had reluctantly acquiesced to international law to allow them in.

Despite all the difficulties, and there were nothing but, my parents after a year and a half managed a convert. One. The bus driver who drove the route to the grocery store six miles away and who had seen my mother dragging me onto her bus every Monday for eighteen months. Hostility turned to grudging turned to gruffness turned to conversation turned to conversion at a painstaking rate, but the first one is always the difficult one. KeithAnne was her name, all seven feet of her, friendly in a frowning sort of way, appalling table manners, but there she was. In the flesh. On a Sunday morning, too big for our inherited American Civil War-era blue Wodehouse tea cups, her fur skirt leaving an uneasy oil across the divan, and a quiver of arrows that I couldn't keep my now-eleven-year-old eyes off of. Nonetheless, a convert.

Consequences were quick to follow.

Why I love who I am

Here, let me give you a list:

1. *The Amazon laugh.* I have worked hard to learn this laugh, and I am getting there. The Amazon laugh is like no other. Rich, deep, uninhibited, superior but happily so. An Amazon will not cover her mouth with her hand when she laughs. She will not form her lips to make vowel sounds of laughter, no 'hoo hoo' or 'hee hee,' only a loud, clanging cataclysm of air, an avalanche of plosives. Her laugh, like so much else Amazonian, is out-and-out warfare. It conquers. It does not comfort. An Amazon laughs like she just created a planet.

   This is all the more impressive because Amazons as a rule have no sense of humour.

2. *Physical Education Class, Year 11.* When the time came to select volleyball teams, the two tallest, most athletic girls in the class, Margo Newman and Sophie Macquarrie-Adler, were chosen by PE Mistress Nobbler as captains. Out of a class of 22, despite being the shortest by over a foot and thumpingly average at volleyball, Margo Newman chose me sixth for her team – the eleventh choice

overall, out of 22 remember – because she thought my 'enthusiasm deserved a chance.' If you need this explained to you, then perhaps you would never understand anyway and should move on to point 3.

3. *The Amazonian Religion.* True, the Amazonian religion, which has no name (another reason to like it), is a bit of an exclusive club. The Goddess, who has no name other than Goddess, demands the supplication of all non-Amazons, and this had led to all sorts of warfare, as you may have noticed. However, if you are an Amazon, and I am, don't forget, all that the Goddess wants for you is your happiness. The Goddess never berates, never punishes. The Goddess is for you and against your enemies. Granted, the being-an-Amazon part is a pretty severe caveat, but if you're in, you're way, way in. As an Amazon, I am not allowed to say more.

4. *HRH, on my fortieth birthday.* Aside from the gifts she gave as Head of State (the silver service, the huge wax seal that I have used ever since for official correspondence), HRH gave me, on the side, in secret, away from official eyes, a butterfly from her gardens. It was an anomaly, she said, a blue Monarch which had slipped in unnoticed in its cocoon on a sequoia she had imported from the UPSA. It was the only blue Monarch in the entire Amazon, HRH told me, holding it lightly between her fingertips. 'Know that it's yours,' she said, and

we watched as she let it fly away free into the flowers of her garden. As a queen, HRH is incapable of friendships. She necessarily has only allies or foes. But, sometimes, she does try.

I do not ask you

Because I have no need to. I know exactly why the CAP depot had enough weapons for a sortie, enough to puncture, blast, and otherwise injure the brave and fierce bodies of our Amazonian soldiers. I also know why only twenty-one soldiers guarded the depot and not the normal complement of fifty-five. I know why the Chartered Accountants moved half of their weapons (because, of course, yes, there were originally more) and more than half of their men only the day before the attack (and for accuracy, since these matters are important for posterity, both for ourselves and for its own sake, all of the CAP soldiers that day were indeed men, whilst all of ours were women; it is not often the stereotypes hold true, but they did that day, making at least an interesting or if not interesting then clarifying footnote in history's own account books). I know, in other words, why the CAP left just enough men to let the depot look protected, though not as many as might have been there, and I know why they left enough arms to make it look fully stocked and ready for war, though again not as many as might have been.

I know because I told them to do this.

The war escalates, as wars will

Most of the early fighting took place in the jungles of Hertfordshire, where our army, that is the Amazonian army (I suppose I don't know for sure who your army might be), was clearly at an advantage. It was swamp fighting of the stickiest, sinkingest, most mosquito-filled type. All brute force, ambushes, and slaughter at no further away than the length of your arm. We naturally excelled and in no time at all the Chartered Accountants were routed, making, if I may say so, a brave last stand in St Albans before it too finally fell to a sky filled with the rapidly finishing arcs of spears and arrows.

The plan, self-evident in its simplicity, was to take the surrounding counties first, leaving the CAP trapped inside the M25. Berkshire, et al would be as easy as Herts for our army. The CAP had never really gotten the hang of jungle-battling and had only received the outlying counties as concession for the Port at Dover (and thereby releasing putative control of the Eurostar tunnel to us) in the Non-Hostilities Pact of 1985. What to do after driving them into Central London was a tougher question. Urban fighting was well within our considerable war talents – had we not taken Manchester and Glasgow from the Vikings? – but the Chartered Accountants lived and breathed urban life, literally. We were good at urban warfare; they were great. So for now, we buckled down, surrounding London, which is no small feat, but then again as the horrendously aged war slogan goes (for we have had many, many, many

wars), 'Amazons are not known for their small feet!'
Are you laughing?

HRH wisely scheduled entertainment for the troops,
including television comediennes, an Irish rap group, and
concert performances of musicals featuring the original
casts from Hove's West End. As I understand it, there
was a *Seven Brides for Seven Brothers* in Watford that
went down a treat.

The missionary work of the ASBCofCinG on the Isle of Man continues, its consequences

So, KeithAnne, who loomed better than anyone I have
ever met, other Amazons included, loomed as in towered,
as in much bigger than, not as in weaving, although I
suspect she probably could have done that as well, we
Amazons being nothing if not multi-skilled. KeithAnne,
our first Amazonian Baptist, the first anywhere as far
as anyone knew and so far last, including yours natur-
alised truly.

Because there were objections you see. Less objections
than anger. Less anger even than outrage, not to put too
fine a point on it, and retribution, brutal and swift.
Missionaries were barely tolerated under international
law but what wasn't tolerated was any degree of success
whatsoever. The Amazonian government, then under a
teenage HRH who therefore may or may not hold
responsibility in any but a titular way, could not of
course sanction what happened to my parents, but once
KeithAnne, in true zealous convert fashion, for there is

no better or at least more eager preacher on earth than the recently born again, began to proselytize to all her co-Amazons, some violent rejoinder was unavoidable.

My poor parents heard nary a mumble of discontent in Jurby East before a window was quietly broken one night and both their throats slit by the hunting knife of an Amazon, who then spared my own life. Why? Only she knows. KeithAnne, besides immediately adopting me, ignoring the pleas of my own government and church, bless her, complained vociferously all the way through the courts, on through the House of Ladies to HRH herself. HRH, while not publicly denouncing the crime, made an offer to welcome me, after a state-funded education and upbringing, into the Amazon race when I reached my adulthood, bless her as well.

So my life changed abruptly. I had a new Amazon mother, new Amazon friends who with disappointing predictability called me 'Shorty' but who also loved me, and a new Amazon outlook on life, one which I grew to embrace passionately. I embrace it even to this day, even after KeithAnne, with typical loving frankness, detailed for me the exact societal circumstances and implications of my parents' deaths, though I can't say I hadn't guessed what had happened but what do you do when handed that news at eleven? As eleven-year-olds in general and eleven-year-old girls in particular are wells of unfocussed anger anyway, I suppose I did the human thing and split it off from myself, built it its own cabinet and locked it away. An unseen fire still gives off heat though, so as much of a love as I have for my race, I still managed to cock one ear when a female CAP operative, having thoroughly researched my history, made a lengthy and subtle offer about information-gathering for the enemy government.

I am a proud Amazon. And I am also a spy against them. You should ask me how that is possible.

The straw that broke the camel's back of Lucia 'Tippi' Ponce-Jones

Of course Amazons have been impressing Chartered Accountants since time immemorial, but for the last hundred years at least, it has been less concubinage than out-and-out relationships which is understandable if perhaps slightly dull. Times change. People modernise. One realises that bludgeoning a man into submission may not perhaps always get you the perfect husband. The Scottish Amazonian Parliament, now that they've realised they can pass a law or two and no one will care or in fact notice, have even formalised an agreement with the Viking governments of Norway and Sweden allowing border perforation for ceremonial Amazon impressments into Scandinavia with reciprocal ceremonial Viking pillagings in the Highlands. Tradition lives on and no one gets hurt. Besides, you have to find a spouse somehow.

Tippi Ponce-Jones, though, was landed gentry, set in due course to become no less than the eleventh Duchess of Shrewsbury, and in those sorts of households the unspoken rules are a bit different. If it had been one of Tippi's younger sisters, Reggie, say, then the current

Duchess, a frightful old piece of stonework named Cosima, might not have cared as much, but as Tippi was future upper crust there were certain procedures to be followed, certain familial pieties to be upheld. Julian Buxton fit nowhere in this.

I have known Cosima Ponce-Jones for twenty years but have disliked her for much longer. She used to be Shadow Culture Secretary in the House of Ladies, a minor post, but no one apparently told Cosima. She was the bane of anything that fell remotely outside of traditional Amazon blood art or wood carving, blasting in her aristocratic gasbag way to the rightwing tabloids about 'Amazonian values', as if 3,000 years of fierceness and pride were endangered by giant plastic children or an ibex in formaldehyde. She was forced to resign after disrupting an extremely popular Noh Theatre Festival in Leicester by garrotting the visiting French director, a matter of finally picking the wrong target.

Tippi, miraculously, was, *is*, a delightful girl. Bright, smart, pretty in a fierce yet bookish sort of way, managing to excel at one of those debutante jobs that are not supposed to involve anything other than smiling and a day or two of filing once a month to make the deb feel like one of the 'people,' whoever they are. She met Accountant Buxton at a diplomatic soiree organised in a sweet irony by her own mother. Let us not mistake the hosting of the party as any indication whatsoever of Cosima Ponce-Jones' politics; she loathed anything foreign in the way that only minor royalty can. Remember though that she was trying to get back in the of course invited HRH's good graces with a view to returning to the House of Ladies by Royal Appointment. As this was the only reason she forced herself to smile widely and think of Amazonia at the blank, pasty faces of the Chartered Accountants who had invaded her home, imagine her horror upon seeing young Tippi sharing a laugh downwards to/with one Mr Buxton, she with nostrils flaring, he with a finger shyly tripping the edge of his wine glass.

Cosima split them up as quickly as diplomacy allowed, sending Tippi on her way bedroomwards and introducing Buxton to the Ladies Brockenwell, the two oldest and most boring twins in the entire UQ. An undaunted Tippi continued inquiries on and then to Mr Buxton through – despite her better judgment – your narrator who is a good friend to have if your mother is unpopular and you want to date a foreigner. Cosima eventually found out, though not about the complicity of yours truly, when happening upon a love letter, of all the romantic, old-fashioned and more to the point completely un-Amazonian things, at least to the Amazons of Cosima's generation.

Family severance was threatened, trust funds were placed into caretakers' hands, Reggie was given Tippi's eldest-sister room. The straw that broke the particular camel's back for Tippi was when Cosima miscalculated again – the woman would be genuinely evil if she weren't so untalented – and mailed an answering letter in Tippi's name to Mr Buxton, ending the relationship and doing her level best to wound him so badly that he wouldn't open further letters or accept future contact.

Why would she think that would work? I'm asking because I genuinely do not know. Sometimes my adopted race is a mystery to me, even after these many years.

Tippi in short order got herself the flat in Slough and made her daring solo raid on the Hemel Palethorpe Gull & Gull annual summer picnic and rounders game. The clubbing with the birthing board wasn't strictly necessary, but by this point, Tippi was caught up in the drama of the thing. Bless her in her ignorance. She couldn't have known the consequences of her actions.

The stupid, naïve, selfish, little cow.

My title incorporates duplicity within itself

HRH often says that the CAP is 'nothing more than a consulate grown malignant' which as with such pronouncements of every world leader in the history of humankind leaves out much more than half the story. To recap: When war broke out in the Belgian Stock Exchange, weak Amazon Queen Jessica XII allowed the democratically elected government, fleeing from certain execution, to take up residence in their London embassy. After the Venture Capitalists won the day in Brussels, Queen Jessica gave up a substantial plot of land to the now-exiled now-former democratically elected government. The CAP was formed and somehow, incredibly, though it probably has most to do with not having to cross either the Channel or the North Sea for impressments, it remained. Various Queens up to and including our own beloved long may she reign HRH have skirmished with it, with varying degrees of success and withdrawal, but all at most with halfheartedness. We don't want the CAP to go anywhere. We like them there. But we also like them to know that we're all around here and that they shouldn't forget it.

It works for everyone.

Except for me. And HRH. But to my eternal regret for different reasons.

My title of Domestic Affairs Advisor incorporates duplicity within itself. The CAP would in the eyes of the world fall under the brief of Dame Geraldine Wiggins, Foreign Affairs Advisor. In the real and far more complicated world in which we are all forced to live, HRH regards the CAP as part of the Amazon, waiting to be reincorporated, and therefore under the purview of the Domestic Affairs Advisor, but secretly so, so that no one would know our intentions.

Which is where I came in.

As promised, HRH kept an eye over my schooling and upbringing. I was given a junior post in government, again appointed rather than elected, and kept in close consultation with HRH. She took a sisterly liking to me as far as she was able (see above for the friendship incapability of monarchs), but there were specific reasons, too. I was an Amazon, but I was not. I was a Manxwoman, but I was not. I was an American, but I was not. Domestic Affairs Advisor, as HRH envisioned it, demanded duplicity, demanded understanding of overt intentions which cloaked covert ones, demanded overall a talent for duality. So, Sally Rae Wentworth at your service. What HRH was not to know was that I was better at my job than she would have wanted or guessed.

Because and yes the war continued, but what the world couldn't know was that HRH was playing this one for keeps. The time had come, now that the Non-Hostilities Pact 1985, negotiated by the CAP Mayor and a high-level Amazonian known only as S (guess), had been called off on the convenient pretext of Tippi Ponce-Jones. The Home Counties taken in a breeze, we commenced border attacks on the M25.

'Yet somehow they always seem to be ready for us,' says HRH, creasing her regal brow. 'Somehow.'

They have asked for an assassination

They have asked for an assassination, which I have of course refused and which only proves how deeply I am misunderstood by both sides. They think my motivation (for what?) is revenge upon the Amazons, which it is but also isn't. I am torn, have always been torn. My eleven-year-old's rage demands a victim, demands a head on a platter as payment for the dance. And yet Amazon blood, which does not in fact run through my veins, nevertheless *runs through my veins*. Am I am who I am, or am I am who I have chosen or rejected, even if I didn't really choose or reject? Because at what point does a person become a people? Did Amazons kill my parents or did an Amazon kill my parents?

The violent deaths of my mother and father did leave their mark, but only in my aversion to violence, an aversion which was built upon the gospel my parents lived and breathed, which KeithAnne, even during the brevity of her exposure to them, embraced and passed along to me.

An aversion to violence. In an Amazon. It would be funny.

I am minimising casualties to as much of an extent as I can by keeping the CAP abreast of our plans, but I am taking lives by prolonging this war, which is not my intention. I could give them enough information to end it, but the cost could very well be too great for the Amazon nation, which is also not my intention. I do not mourn or pick over my betrayal because the very savagery of my own soldiers that I see in day-to-day operations convinces me that my actions are right, and yet I do mourn and pick over my betrayal because that savagery is the vibrant lifeblood of the world that has raised me, has made me as much as possible one of their own. I am an Amazon, and I am not. I am both, and I am neither.

Surely, I am that most worthless of idealists, stuck on the fence, paralysed and useless, unable to act or able to act only in ways that are opposite to what I believe. How do you get here if all the work you do is to not get here?

And then despite the best efforts of your narrator

We made a great stride forward. Moving up from Wimbledon and down from Harrow, we swiftly beat the

CAP army back through the West End and, despite heavy fighting in the City, on out into the East End. The CAP government is now holed up in Hackney, its demise inevitable and imminent. Over 16,000 CAP troops died, along with over 31,000 Amazons, the greater skill at urban warfare giving CAP the greater impact if not the victory. The Great Feast is now crowded and boisterous well beyond belief.

HRH smiled cryptically at me today. I wonder if I was able to hide my surprise at our stride forward quickly enough.

I have been summoned

I walk through the Palace, holding my head up, feeling a deep calm that exists only because fear by this time has become pointless. I have failed, though failure implies a cohesive aim, which I do not have and never had. I have dissembled. I have been unable to reconcile. Despite and because of my best efforts, people have died, the war has continued, is almost won. A people whom I love and hate, persons whom I only love. Perhaps there really is no end to this division. So the CAP are nearly conquered, but will HRH discover that I have been right for the wrong reasons? Who are the Amazons without an enemy? How can you take away war from those you love when taking away war would cause them to cease being the person that you love? I have reached forty-seven, and the waters remain muddied.

I will not reach forty-eight, it seems.

The room is warm as I enter, and unguarded. Why should they need guards when they are Amazons, and I am not? The elected Cabinet sit in a half-circle with HRH at the centre. They all look at me, stern, though they are always stern. I ignore them and study only the face of HRH. Is disappointment there? Is anger? My thirty years of friendship cannot overcome her lifetime of Royal training. I am unable to read her gaze.

She waits for a moment, and then she speaks.

'Sally Rae?' she says and, yes, it is definitely a question.

the Seventh International Military War Games
Dance Committee Quadrennial Competition
and Jamboree

Gone to Blazes?

Caught in a miasma of accusations of cheating, 'excessive' casualties, and an increasing championing of athleticism over artistry, the International Military War Games Dance Committee Quadrennial Competition and Jamboree finds itself suffering an identity crisis on the eve of Opening Ceremonies in Ottawa. **Sharon Huckabee** reports

Irena Sultanova of Ukraine lines up for another quadruple Salchow, a move unheard of in this event until American Stephanie Butts-Liberty completed the first successful one eight years ago at the Fifth Competition in Gdansk, earning herself the Ice Dancing and Shooting gold in the process. Six of the seven top contenders here this year include a quad Salchow in their routine; the seventh, Marianne Jouvert of Switzerland, is expected to *finish* seventh.

Sultanova, last Competition's silver-medallist and this year's favorite for gold, gathers speed, whizzes by front-row spectators at what seems an alarmingly dangerous velocity, reaches her takeoff point near the rink's far end, whips herself up into the air, spins one two three yes four times, and manages to get off three shots from her Kalashnikov as she lands. The rotation of her spin is too fierce though: one shot finds its target in an effigy of Tsar Nicolas II, but another splinters wood along the far barrier, and the third hits a janitor sweeping seats way up in the fifteenth row.

As the janitor receives medical attention, Sultanova heaves a deep sigh, reloads her rifle, and lines up for another attempt. 'It's a stupidly hard jump,' she will tell me later, deep bags under her eyes. 'This is supposed to be ice-*dancing*. Tell me, where is it dancing when you just *fling* yourself into the air as hard as you can, huh?'

This, however, is all the dissent I'll hear from young Miss Sultanova because her coach soon arrives. He's the controversial

203

Icelandic Haldor Gudmundsson who not only guided Butts-Liberty to gold two Competitions ago but also managed gold and silver at the Sixth Competition with, respectively, Germany's Edwina Kschwendt (now deceased), and Sultanova. He immediately sends the defending silver medallist to her dressing room and provides his own version of her opinion.

'She is much tired,' he says, lighting a second cigarette while one still smolders in the corner of his mouth. 'She say big, grumpy thing. She not mean it. What she *mean* is that she excited for competition and that quadruple Salchow has taken Women's Ice Dancing And Shooting to whole new level.'

I ask Gudmundsson about Sultanova's point that 'flinging yourself in the air as hard as you can' can hardly be called *dancing*.

'What is this *dancing* that everyone wants so much?' asks Gudmundsson, waving his hands in the air, two cigarettes now hanging from his lower lip. 'You call it dancing if you want but IMWGD also want an athletics competition. So which is it? I ask you. You can have arts, or you can have sports. You cannot have both.'

IMWGD, the International Military War Games Dance Committee – Gudmundsson pronounces this, as do all the competitors here, as a rueful joke: 'I'm wigged' – would pretend to be appalled to hear a coach dismiss the Competition's artistic aims so effortlessly. But Gudmundsson isn't finished. He proceeds to tick off other events in this year's Competition:

'You try to tell me that the Singles and Doubles Tumbling and Bayoneting routines are *dancing*? If you say that, I say you are blind. That is *not* dancing. That is gymnastics with gunplay, nothing more. The Cheerleading and Tactical Competition? Bah! What's going to get you a higher score, huh? That you kill more of the opposing teams than anyone else or that you don't mess up your cheers as you die?'

Off the record, even IMWGD officials concede that Gudmundsson has a point. Fatalities at this year's event are expected to exceed the last Competition's record total of 741. Forty-seven countries have pulled out of the Tap and Jazz Events after an Australian entrant was allowed to enter with an Uzi, something the protestors – keen to keep the competition single-action – are

A Stab at Interactivity

In a bid to combat what it sees as a 'plateau-ing' audience share over the last two Competitions, NBC has introduced *Bang!*, a tele-video interactive available over their digital cable hook-ups.

'It's fantastic!' says NBC President Vivika Summers. 'You've got all the regular digital interactive features – athlete information, Competition history and so forth – but for the first time, you'll actually be able to compete against real Competition athletes in online gaming!'

The intended big draw is that the online gaming culminates in the redundantly titled *BangBang!*, in which the top online gamers from around the world will be brought to Ottawa for a special live ammunition final. The overall winner receives $50,000, and NBC will provide $10,000 to the families of all non-winners.

---

calling 'legal to the letter of the law, but not the spirit of the Competition'. And the ice dancers, tiny Irena Sultanova included, are risking hip dislocation and permanent disability in pursuit of ever more difficult jumps that turn alleged dance moves into inelegant struggles against dismemberment.

After 24 years, and on the eve of the Seventh Competition, has the world's largest and most popular international war games dance event lost its way?

Ideals That Surprised Everyone By Working

As envisioned by its founder, Jackson Grant Lincoln VI, the ebullient if short-tempered former Governor of Tennessee, the Competition is 'a place for the world to set aside its politics and historic rivalries, and to compete against each other in fair and equitable war games dancing competitions, held under the banner of international freedom and with the aim of as little excessive bloodshed as possible.'

No one, of course, upon hearing such idealistic sentiment – spoken by Lincoln at the Opening Ceremonies of the First Competition – took them at face value, especially not after Lincoln himself became one of the First Competition's 134 fatalities. (He was killed in an accidental grenade blast while competing in the Wheelchair Formation Drills, though the American team did go on to win gold, dedicating their victory to Lincoln's memory.) The general assumption was that countries would, as they had on the world's battlefields, use the dance provisions of the Treaty of Versailles and the Geneva Convention as cover for all manner of aggression and atrocity.

But then a strange thing happened. The First Competition's very first event was Modern Interpretive Artillery (Light-Armoured Division). After an incident-less opening round (Finland v Malta), the world held its collective breath as Israel faced Syria in a randomly selected match-up. Would Israel unveil its long-rumored handheld smart bombs and use the opportunity to vaporize eight fit Syrians? Would Syria, as also long-rumored, base its routine on a day in the life of a suicide bomber and not only obliterate itself but the Israeli team as well?

Tensions were high. The audience removed itself to a safe distance. The music began (Kander & Ebb's 'Two Ladies'), and dancing commenced. Four minutes and thirty-one seconds later, it was finished, with only a single Syrian casualty so clearly and artfully within the rules that the Syrian coach publicly shook the hand of the Israeli coach. The dancers and coaches had taken the Competition seriously as a *competition*, not as a further excuse for more war. Maybe Jackson Lincoln had a point after all.

And aside from a few infamous incidents (the Chilean germ-warfare 'accident' of the Third Competition; the short-lived Canadian fashion of choreographed self-genocide in the Fifth), the Competition has remained broadly true to Lincoln's founding sentiments of providing a place for international fairness and healthy competitive spirit. Which makes it all the more ironic that the greatest current complaint about the Competition is that it has now become *too* competitive, losing all sense of fun and beauty in the quest for gold, gold, gold.

Keeping Things Heep

IMWGD's President disagrees. As he does with most things.

'The Competition, it evolves,' debonair and surprisingly tiny President Argento Conetti tells me later in the tasteful offices rented for him in Ottawa's premier business district for the duration of the Seventh Competition. 'Just like society has evolution. Things are, eh, how you say, *sharper* in the world than in Jackson Lincoln's day. They could afford things to be a little fuzzier then, more, eh, the expression in English is "laid-back", I believe. Now, you have hundreds and hundreds of channels on the television dedicated to war sports, not just dancing. You've got film festivals and rival competitions that, eh, gather to themselves the impression of hipness.'

Conetti pronounces this *heepness*, and it is a theme to which he warms. 'Heepness, fair or not, is what the Competition *must* keep up with if it is to survive. We cannot be accused of being un-heep or that is the end of us, no? We must be as heep as the next fellow and so that maybe means the Competition gets tougher. It gets faster and harder. Okay, okay, okay, so maybe *some* of the artistry suffers maybe a leetle, but if that is the price for heepness, than I am willing to cough it up.'

'Faster and harder' the Competition certainly is. Take the Synchronised Swimming Subterfuge, as a random example. In the First Competition, Sweden won gold with a four-minute routine to Handel's 'For Unto Us A Child Is Born' in which their high marks for artistic perfection overcame low technical marks for only up-ending four of six target mini-submarines. In the last Competition, the US team scored gold for a *ninety-second* routine to 'Lady Marmalade' in which they achieved middling artistic scores but a set of perfect technicals for exploding *eighteen* full-size floating mines with potassium grenades. Much like the ice dancing, more artistic routines barely got a look in. Faster and harder, indeed.

Critics blame this dominance of technical perfection over artistic aims on three key developments that seem to be coming to a head in this year's Competition:

Exhibit One: Cheating, Letter vs. Spirit

As already mentioned, 47 countries have removed themselves from this Competition's Tap and Jazz Events after Australian Jason Coolibah won the right to use a multi-shot Uzi. The event is described in the Competition's bylaws as 'a classic event taken directly from the battlefields of World War I in which contestants display the beauty and poetry of tap and jazz in hand-to-hand combat.' This was interpreted for the first six Competitions as limiting the event to single-shot handguns. Coolibah pointed out that the rules only list maximum measurements for barrel length and contain no actual reference to single-action guns.

Despite cries of this being unsportsmanlike – in the Australian National Qualifiers, Coolibah won a place on the international team after killing *every single one* of his fellow single-action competitors in the *first round* – the Competition Steering Committee reluctantly admitted that Coolibah was correct. He and his Uzi have been allowed to proceed, but since every other country in the world had only had single-action qualifying rounds to find their own competitors, no one else stands a chance, hence the mass withdrawal. Only very small countries like Benin and French Guiana remain, hoping to earn themselves posthumous silvers and bronzes.

'Tap and jazz in the *Eighth* Competition is going to be one quick, boring bloodbath,' complains one of the withdrawing contestants.

This is not an isolated case. There was a similar uproar at the last Competition over Bulgaria's

No Nukes! Yet.

What IMWGD *hasn't* allowed this year is the use of so-called 'body nukes', small, shoulder-mounted launchers used to fire low-payload, specifically-targeted nuclear weapons.

'There *are* limits,' says Doctor Conetti. 'I don't think anyone would seriously consider body nukes sportsmanlike.'

Nevertheless, up to seven unidentified countries (thought to include the US, Iran, and Luxembourg) filed formal requests for their use.

'We just can't get the insurance,' says Conetti. 'Besides, you'd need a playing field of about 400 square kilometres that you'd never be able to use again. Ottawa has declined to agree to such a request.'

Maybe next Competition in Kuala Lumpur, then?

'I have no comment at this time,' says Conetti.

use of a tank in Cheerleading and Tactical, and this year, there have been complaints about Japan's laser-guidance systems in the Salsa Single Elimination event.

'What's the point of feeling the music in your soul if all you're able to do is put off death for an extra ten or fifteen seconds?' asks defending Salsa gold-medallist Karen Cupitt, who retired over the summer after losing her sixth partner in three years to competitive fatalities. 'It's just stopped being any fun.'

Exhibit Two: Amateur vs. Professional

The Competition was started as a meeting place for the world's best amateur war games dancers, intending to catch college competitors before they entered the lucrative professional leagues, but this division began to blur early on. Members of the US Professional Ballroom Martial Arts League, the world's most profitable professional sports league, were naturally banned from the First Competition. However, members of the Chinese BMAL *were* allowed to compete as that League was state-run and therefore, arguably, still amateur since no one profited.

Then, in the Fourth Competition, Armament Actors Equity argued that its members should be allowed to participate in the mime events, pointing out that India had been allowed to enter several Bollywood stars only because India's equivalent actors' union did not have a mime division and therefore the otherwise professional actors were, according to a loophole, only amateur mimes.

The floodgates were opened. The USPBMAL had its members competing in the very next Competition and nearly every event this year is filled with various levels of world professionals in every conceivable permutation. The athletes argue that this is merely a levelling of the playing field, but there can be little doubt the Competition loses some of its naive charm when the man you're rooting for on the High Dive Napalm Springboard is already a millionaire many times over.

Exhibit Three: The Increase of Casualties

Much has been made of the increase in fatalities at the Competition over the years, but this complaint is perhaps the one that is least justifiable. While it is true that the raw number of deaths has invariably increased over the years – from 134 in the First Competition to an estimated 1,000 this year – the number of athletes participating has also increased: nearly 11,000 are expected to be here this year as opposed to just 1,685 at the First Competition (see chart). The percentage of athletes killed has actually stayed at a fairly steady eight per cent.

'That's still an awful lot of people killed,' says Patricia Merton, head of War No Dance Yes, the largest (if faintly heeded) protest group against the very concept of the Competition.

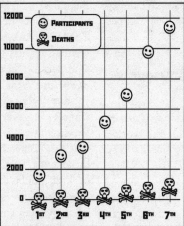

'I mean, how can you sit there with a straight face and tell me that the 1,000 people expected to die in this year's Competition is acceptable because it's part of a historic percentage? Can you even hear what you're saying?'

Minority pressure groups aside, it is generally agreed by Competition experts that the perception of the continually escalating body count is worse than the actual fact of it.

'What happens,' says Hugh Echo, a seasoned Competition broadcaster and commentator, 'is that the *perception* of need for a high body count takes over, and I think that *is* something to be wary of. Fatalities are meant to happen with a heavy heart and with artistic import. I'd start to worry if they became something to aim for for their own sake, rather than just the by-product of a natural competitive spirit. I do wonder if that's the hidden reason behind a lot of these new weapons and tactics, and not just a natural need to excel.'

The Seventh Competition will be watched carefully, and if the fatality count exceeds the eight per cent threshold, President Conetti has promised to look at the current rules. 'If the fatalities get too high then, yes, I guess, who will be left to compete in future games?' he tells me while staring out his office window. 'We don't want to get to a point where it is more than just the chaff getting eliminated.'

Whither the Jamboree?

'Oh, God!' shouts Conetti, 'Don't come to me about the Jamboree! If I could get rid of it, I would! The world would be a better place!'

The Jamboree, never the most popular part of the Competition, has this year been completely delegated to a single evening's 'entertainment', broadcast on the very minor Midwestern Family Love cable network. Conetti puts his head in his hands at the thought of it. 'All those awful cheeldren dancing around with banners and plastic rifles,' he moans.

In addition to the 'awful cheeldren', this year's line-up boasts Cliff Richard, Gloria Estefan, and the Beach Boys. 'Don't look at me,' says Conetti, 'I didn't plan it.' Instead, he's taken the mildly controversial decision of selling the rights to a production company for a flat fee. 'Let them take the burden and good riddance.'

Jerry Spong, the president of Falderol Productions, the company that paid that flat fee, puts a brave face on things. 'Well, Dr Conetti is an athlete, let's not forget,' he says with a permanently toothy smile. 'We get a lot of flack from the competitors for being just a fun little party for the kids but hey, it's tradition.'

It is indeed. Competition Founder Lincoln envisioned the Jamboree as a 'fun, family show to inspire future generations of Competitors'. In reality, this has meant brightly dressed platoons of elementary school children waving banners of pastel crêpe paper while ill-matched former stars performed ill-conceived duets. Remember Mickey Mouse and Brooke Shields from the First Competition? Who would have thought it would be downhill from there?

'Okay, I admit there have been some low points,' says an unabashed Spong. 'I personally would never have put Pavarotti and Matt LeBlanc in koala suits, for example,' referring to the particularly derided Sixth Competition's Jamboree in Melbourne, widely believed to be the trigger for Pavarotti's subsequent retirement from performing. 'Although the ratings on that were very high in young demographics even so.'

Conetti fully admits that the

selling of the Jamboree to cable is an attempt to bring the viewing figures below the ratings threshold set in the Competition Charter that will allow him to cancel it once and for all. Spong is optimistic that they'll easily beat the required twenty share, but with a trained performing moose taking centre stage to symbolise this year's celebration of Ottawa, the outlook is unsure at best.

'It's family fun,' says Spong. 'Tat!' screams Conetti. 'Dreck! Unwatchable keetsch!'

The Future?

Despite all these complaints, Conetti and indeed most of the competitors still unironically swear that they expect this year's Competition to be the best.

'11,000 competitors performing their hearts out,' pleads an impassioned President. 'What more could you want?'

Haldor Gudmundsson agrees: 'It's still the biggest, you know? Yes, you have all those smaller versions, the Commonwealth War Games and what have you, but you just ask anyone here whether they'd have a Commonwealth Gold or a Competition Gold. The man who says Commonwealth is a liar.'

And so Irena Sultanova lines herself up for another go at flinging her body into the air as hard as she can. If it's a less artistic jump than whoever wins the silver medal, then maybe that's no longer the point. I watch as she gathers speed and makes her attempt, this time nailing the jump beautifully, landing perfectly, but still hitting only one target out of three.

'Not good enough!' screams Gudmundsson from the coach's bench.

Let the Competition, for better or worse, commence.

the gifted

WE ARE GHOSTS HERE, TELLING this story. We will not make it to the end. We would like you to know this up front, because it is exactly the sort of thing we, as a group, would have delighted in telling you ahead of time, with serious and concerned looks on our faces, before our circumstances changed as they did, before we became simply these voices with a story to tell.

We would have wanted you to like us. We realise now that we probably would have failed.

'LET'S SEE,' SAID MISS PRIVET, 'shovels and spades. Picks, brushes, rakes, spoons, gloves. I think that's it. Are we ready?'

All together we said, 'Yes, Miss Privet.'

The digging could at last begin on Phase 1.

MEMORIES WITHIN MEMORIES. THE STORY comes to us in a rush, all its bits and pieces simultaneous as is the way with things here. It is difficult, even for us, even with the resources we brought to this place, to keep from vomiting it on you all at once. We've never wished to be an inconvenience, and we will try our best not to be so now. But this story is two stories: the story of how we got here, of course, which is easy as everyone remembers their journey, but it is also the more difficult story of who we were.

Who were we?

We were Group A (we were), and we, under the

leadership of Dagmar Hewson-Hill, 12, had chosen equality as our over-riding theme, which was a predictable, teacher-pleasing gambit that fooled no one, not even ourselves. Dagmar, nascent feminist, nascent crusader, nascent woman, was the tallest in Group A, also the most interested, also the most vocal, and so our natural leader. She was the focal point for the gang of us that had coalesced, almost unconsciously, almost so that emotionally eagle-eyed Miss Privet didn't even notice, into our usual playground clique when Miss Privet had instructed us to split ourselves into a Group A and a Group B four weeks before the digging. We were, naturally, separate from our class's other obvious group.

'Isn't it possible,' Miss Privet had said, smiling the kindly, twitchy, slightly sarcastic smile of a young earnest adult compelled by instinct to supervise children and about to say in ironic tones that we had done something terribly disappointing but not to bother ourselves about it too much, 'that we could have a little more diversity within Groups A and B? Remember when we talked about diversity? Remember how I wrote ho-mo-gen-e-i-ty *and* het-er-o-gen-e-i-ty *on the board? Remember . . .' She sighed. 'Never mind,' she said. 'This is supposed to be fun.'*

And so our normal group, our customary half of the class, became officially Group A, and Group B formed of the usual herd of hangers-on that surrounded Jasper Wheeler like big, fat, black bees casting themselves on the leaves of a dying flower.

'Thank you, Miss Privet,' said Dagmar and Jasper, looking directly at one another.

'This is Group A's area,' said Miss Privet, opening her scarily bony arms to indicate a tree-enclosed glen. 'You can start marking out your quadrants and getting burial depths as soon as the rest of us leave. I believe we all know what to do, yes?'

'Yes,' said Dagmar and a fair portion of the rest of us in Group A. We were eager to begin.

'You might have a little trouble with tree roots,' said Miss Privet to audibly impatient shuffling from some of the more intense-eyed members of our group, 'but I think this a good spot.'

'Yes, Miss Privet,' said Dagmar, the sharpness in her voice only barely disguised. This was finally the fun part after four weeks – *four weeks!* – of classroom work.

'Okay, then.' Miss Privet smiled. 'We'll leave you to it.' She loved nothing more than to see us excited to be learning, when in fact we were far more excited at the opportunity to demonstrate our maturity at being allowed to work at least partially unsupervised. 'Group B, follow me!'

Miss Privet walked out of the trees, heading towards a spot a couple of hundred yards off where Group B would start their digging out of sight and earshot of Group A.

'Good luck,' Jasper Wheeler said, lingering behind. Overt sneering would have been too obvious. The simple 'good luck' let us know exactly where Jasper Wheeler thought we stood.

'I don't think we're going to need any luck,' said Dagmar, unflinching.

'Come on, Jasper,' called Miss Privet from a harmless distance. 'Time's a-wasting.'

'So it is,' said Jasper, quietly, watching us as he left. 'So it is.'

WHO WERE WE? WE WERE *half of the Gifted Project, a shifting inexact title thrust upon our welcoming heads, thirty of us in the class in total, and a group as dispiritingly homogeneous as Miss Privet's dearest left-wing nightmares.*

To a student, we were middle-class at least, with two parents or one parent and one variously selected co-parent who, as a rule, read to us at home while working professional non-blue-collar jobs (doctor, patent lawyer, orchestral arranger) that nonetheless allowed them to lavish attention and interaction upon us. These parental figures of ours never swore at us, rarely yelled, and when we were bad, were 'disappointed' and never, ever 'pissed off'. They never struck us, always fed us, regularly trumpeted our achievements. We had been stimulated as infants (classical music and poetry played for us in the womb), allowed to read in corners as our independence developed, taken to zoos and theatres, even the occasional opera, taught to cook simple meals when we expressed curiosity and encouraged to turn household chores into various games. We usually had interesting and/or conscientious grandparents. We were smart, yes, some of us scarily so, but we'd had the added benefit of homes that made us bright, too.

And so when we attended regular schools with regular pupils, we were bored out of our little minds. School was much *less stimulating than the sensual primary-color pleasures of the homes that our entitled parents – so nervous not to* over-discipline, *so keen not to stifle – had provided for us. We were the most demanding pupils in our respective classes dotted around the Tacoma Public School District: of attention, of motivation, of extra sensory input. We had already read all the books our teachers recited in patronising tones to circles of our dumbstruck classmates. We already had years of finger-painting and papier-maché experience under our 14-inch belts. We found the songs of the sing-alongs unchallenging and insufficiently polyphonic.*

All of which was enough for an eager school district to use us to inaugurate its new 'gifted' program for especially talented youngsters in that deadest year of our childhoods, 1982. And so we were to be whisked away from our classmates, like farmers in flying saucers, and dropped off in the brightly lit, innovatively-laid-out classroom of tall, wiry-haired, Miss Privet, a woman desperate to mold us, desperate to encourage a clutch of geniuses, and often just desperate. Perfect for a pilot program, then.

An unknown civil servant, however, came up with a humane and terrible idea, a wrinkled caveat to the new gift of our extraordinariness. We were all to be retrieved by a gifted bus from our gifted homes scattered around the huge, urban school district and driven miles and miles and miles to Plisterfeld Elementary, the poorest school in the entire city. Not just poor, it was the main elementary school for the dilapidated housing project that surrounded and engulfed it, meaning that its students were invariably the poorest of those poor, often the children of adults with less learning and coping ability than the new crop of thirty students bussed in from points opulent. Even our inexperienced 10-, 11- and 12-year-old brains could see that this was a bad idea, in fact the worst of ideas, not because we were afraid of the underprivileged students – though we were – but because we were instantly, despite the best of intentions, a reminder of exactly how underprivileged the under-privileged were. Even in our extreme youth, perhaps without even knowing the word, we could tell we were thirty living, breathing examples of civic condescension.

We were hated. Immediately. Plisterfeld loathed us with a surprisingly creative passion. Sudden brutal turf wars at recess left us sequestered under the rusted monkey bars near the far fence. Lunches in the cafeteria so often ended in mashed burgers, spilt milk, and tears that we were eventually allowed to eat in our own class-room. School assemblies were a rain of spitballs from behind and a surging tide of farts from the front. If it felt like we were under siege, it was because we were. We even noticed that Miss Privet, young, gender-neutral, full of new ideas, was snubbed by the other teachers, save the thousand-year-old Mrs Giberson, who was far too senile to notice that Miss Privet was rightly regarded as an untouchable.

We didn't blame them. We were too patronising for that. We merely gave each other deeply felt speeches about how difficult it must be and how hard their daily lives no doubt were what with all of their fathers in jail and all of their mothers alcoholic and all of them clearly subjected to daily abuse by ominous visiting 'stepdads'. We swelled our hearts with pity and avoided them like the plague.

If anyone had asked any of the children on either side of this miniature Cold War, eloquent denunciations of the adult-sponsored plan could have been easily provided. Children are, though, the last to be consulted on issues of their own welfare, so our opinions went unheard. Besides, the adults thought this was a brilliant idea, one celebrating the 'specialness' of Plisterfeld, one indicating that the elected School Board played no favorites among the disparate income levels across the sprawling district. And of course, once you so publicly give something to the poor, you can never take it back, no matter how disastrous its effects.

We were therefore a world unto our own, ostracised by the other students and left to our own paltry defenses. This should have inspired solidarity among us, a herd instinct in which we should have thrived against adversity.

It didn't. It inspired two solidarities, separate ones. And in any system of two competing herds fighting for the same territory, co-existence is never possible. One herd must always vaniquish, and one herd must always be vanquished.

OUR FIRST TASK WAS MARKING our burial site with a string border and then further string quadrants within that border. Pratip Mukherji, our designated string-layer, was poised to begin. Taking our cue from Dagmar, though, no one moved until Miss Privet and Group B had completely disappeared behind a series of low rises and trees. We waited a beat more, listening to the chirps of birds and rustlings of pine needles.

The digging sites were located in a mysterious wooded area behind the school. We were never fully informed as to the exact nature of the area, only that it was normally forbidden for students to trespass there. Miss Privet, backed no doubt by a School Council frantic for its Gifted Project to make some kind of heretofore unseen breakthrough, won permission for us to dig there. It appeared to be some division of the housing project abandoned in early construction. There was a paved, looping road and concrete driveways, but no houses. There were one or two foundations, but it seemed as if the government had suddenly run out of money or motivation. The roads, driveways and foundations were left, and nature had returned, tall trees growing up where kitchens were supposed to have been, raspberry bushes instead of lawns. It was an eerie place, with the feeling of a world after the human race had died.

We loved it. It was spooky, the right kind of spooky, meaning brightly lit.

'All right,' said Dagmar, taking a deep breath, her brow deeply serious. 'Lay the string, Pratip.'

As GROUP A, WE WERE – *though not at all racially – the unspoken white group. The unsoiled, untainted group, if you will, but not in any physical or wealthy way. We were not any cleaner than those in the other group, nor of any special privilege that they lacked, nor of any higher economic strata.*

We were the precocious group that knew what adults wanted to hear from children they regarded as intelligent, and we fed them those lines regularly and without hesitation. We were so good at this, so eager to please, such obvious toadies pandering to comfortable grown-up expectations that we sometimes disgusted ourselves. To select one example among many: when asked in Sunday School class to make a list of his favorite activities, Robbie Normer, one of a number of tow-headed members in our group, not only wrote down 'concentrating' as his most favorite activity, he then asked his Sunday School teacher Mrs Asbjornsen if he had spelled it correctly. This was not because he in any way suspected that he had misspelled it, but because he wanted to be sure that Mrs Asbjornsen noticed and paid due attention to the fact that he not only knew the word 'concentrating' at such a tender age but also professed to do it in large and self-entertaining quantities. When Robbie confessed to us at school the next day, quite redfaced at what he had done, Tom Hulver said, 'You should have just been honest and put down playing with yourself.'

Because, you see, our precocity did not extend to when we were on our own. We regarded that precocity as an act deployed on easily manipulated adults to get what we wanted. It was shameful, it was dirtying, it was felt to be beneath our true talents and skills, but as a group, it got us places. Miss Privet's gifted class with liberal unsupervised learning modules, for one.

Jasper Wheeler's group was nothing like us. We didn't understand Jasper Wheeler's group at all.

* * *

AFTER PRATIP LAID THE STRING in suitable quadrants, Dagmar redeployed our digging instruments so that strength was matched with strength, so that we all became equivalent diggers.

'That shovel is too big for you, Terry,' she said. Terry Yotter (and the name helped not at all) was the class androgyne, and we had gone an amazing eleven days at the beginning of our first school year together before Tom Hulver finally worked up the nerve to directly verify Terry's gender (male, though it really was impossible to tell since Terry wore big hair, thick glasses and baggy clothes that made it seem as if he was trying to use his own body as a hermitage). 'Take David's spade and give the shovel to Chris. Linda, you give your rake to David and take Chris' brushes.'

'But I want to dig with the rake,' said Linda Zhang, our skinny-but-growing second-generation Chinese representative who was forced to practice three hours a day on a cello twice her size by parents with specific ideas about How to Excel in the Land of Opportunity.

'Your mom and dad don't like you to get your arms too tired.'

'But you let me swing on the monkey bars at recess.'

Dagmar smiled patiently. 'This is much harder than monkey bars. You know Miss Privet will get another letter if your arms run out of steam when you're practicing tonight.' Dagmar rubbed Linda's shoulder sympathetically. 'You can lay out the artefacts when it's time.'

'Thanks, Dagmar.'

'No need to thank me,' said Dagmar. 'We're a democracy, remember? The work is divided equally.'

'Can we start already?' said Tom Hulver.

'There's no need to wait for me,' said Dagmar, in a tone just slightly too instructive. We forgave her when she picked up her own shovel.

THE ASSIGNMENT WAS INTENDED TO *teach us about archeology and ancient civilizations. Since textbooks were clearly not interesting or stimulating or exciting enough for us gifteds, and filmstrips and videos insufficiently cutting-edge (played, as they were, on a massive early 80s tank VCR that seemed straight from a newsroom with its top-loading cartridges and array of small plastic tabs), it was clear that something revolutionary needed to be done lest our brains atrophy from boredom. We remain, even in our present state when such things should no longer be a mystery, unaware of whether the idea came from Miss Privet, a modern teaching guide or an invisible curriculum committee somewhere, but for once, we did not mind. The idea was blindingly good.*

In order to find out not only how archeologists recovered rare artefacts and reconstructed dead civilizations but also to inflame our imaginations about the day-to-day existence of those civilizations and to throw a bit of mythology and a bit of art class into the mix, we were asked to do nothing less than actually create *a civilization with its own overriding themes, its own laws and traditions and beliefs, and most importantly, its own artefacts.*

'Artefacts have power,' said Miss Privet, in an uncharacteristically metaphysical moment. 'They're the *crystallization of everything that the civilization was, of everything the civilization thought about itself. Don't underestimate the sort of magic and history that is contained in a relic.'*

'But these will be fake,' said Jasper Wheeler.

'That's not quite the point, Jasper. You're creating a whole civilization, and the artefacts you create will be a concentration of all your imaginings about it.' She seemed lost in some sort of teacherly reverie. 'I want you all to keep in mind that you're not just making bowls or paintings. You're representing entire worlds, entire peoples. Fictional or not, it doesn't matter.'

'And these things have power?' asked Jasper, pen poised.

Miss Privet shrugged a friendly shrug with the look of a woman in the ecstasy of really connecting and interfacing with her students. 'A kind of power, yes, I think so. All the power of an entire people filtered down to one object. It could be very powerful.'

The genius of the project was that the class would split into two equal-sized groups (of which there has already been some discussion) who would each design a civilization and construct various artefacts and ruins from it. The nature of the civilization each group created was to remain secret from the other group, because the artefacts would then be buried in separate plots. Each group (and this is the part we loved so much) would then switch plots, dig up the other group's artefacts and attempt to reconstruct their civilization based on those artefacts. After a week's analysis, reports would be written and presentations made before the entire class.

We would then be graded on how well we had guessed the civilization the other group had created.

We were not particularly worried about the actual grades. We were gifted students and invariably either got top marks or offers of counselling to help us get top marks. What we were interested in was how well we could flummox the other group, how well we could disguise our intentions from Jasper Wheeler and his ilk. There were, of course, strict guidelines from Miss Privet as it would have been all too easy to make the artefacts impossible to guess. We were required to give the other group a fair chance, making this war all the more appealing as it would have to be undercover.

Jasper Wheeler seemed to feel the same. Even on that first day, even before we had officially split into two separate (though preordained) groups, he and his Jasperlings had looked over at us with excited opportunity on their faces. 'This is the best idea you've ever had, Miss Privet,' he said, ignoring her completely.

Miss Privet actually blushed. 'Why, thank you, Jasper,' she said. 'That's very sweet.' And she obviously meant it, poor woman.

WE DUG. ACCORDING TO THE rules of the project, we could go no deeper than eighteen inches. Any further would have made it too difficult for the other group to find our artefacts. We, of course, were hoping we could dig down six or even ten feet, but we soon discovered that digging down eighteen inches in a fifteen-by-eight-foot rectangle was more work than we and perhaps even Miss Privet could have imagined.

Somehow, somewhere along the line of this project, we had all decided to wear khaki shorts for the dig, some of us even buying new pairs for the occasion. There had been no discussion about it, but we were all also wearing minor variations on a light-blue, long-sleeved digging shirt. None of us had ever mentioned wearing the same shirt, but there it was, an impromptu uniform that made us look like a real team.

As we slowly, laboriously removed an impossible amount of dirt and still only managed a depth of infuriatingly gradual inches, Larry Patmos and Linda Zhang began plotting out exactly where our artefacts were going to go. We had an original plan of course, but tree roots, immovable boulders (including one the size of a labrador) and an unexpected stripe of rusted plumbing we were afraid to touch, all required some modification to our blueprints. We buried our small symbolically-painted chariot along the eastern wall of the shallow pit to emphasise its relation to the rising sun. We put our mosaic right side up in the fingers of a tree root and placed the various scales at each of the four corners. The manuscripts were set alongside the rusted piping at regular intervals to make it look like we had planned for the piping all along. Deepest of all, we buried our Rosetta stone, the bit that would unlock the rest of the artefacts, in a mischievously devised cavern dug out from underneath the concrete foundation.

'They're never going to find that,' said Richie Goldstein, the one of us who got car-sick on every field trip.

'I know,' said Dagmar, savouring the thought. 'They'll –'

'How's it going, campers?' Miss Privet's voice boomed through our little glade like an invasion force.

'Very, very well, Miss Privet,' said Dagmar.

Miss Privet stopped. 'You're allowed to say *cool*, Dagmar,' she said, the look on her face pleading for us to be her friend. 'Or *awesome*. Or *tubular*.' Stifled laughter from Pratip and David Middleton. Miss Privet gave them a look. 'Or whatever words you use among yourselves.'

Dagmar looked slightly put out. 'But it *is* going very, very well, Miss Privet.'

'Yes, but you don't have to *say* it like that. You don't have to be so formal, Dagmar. This is fun. You're allowed to act like it's fun.'

Dagmar made sideways glances at Tom Hulver and Terry Yotter. 'Thank you very much, Miss Privet,' she said. 'We'll all do our best to keep that in mind.'

THERE WERE MORE WAYS IN *which we, the gifted, were different than the normal run of things in the Tacoma Public School District. Apparently, and it really did seem incredible even then, despite there being over 18,000 students in the greater Tacoma metropolitan area, the requirements were so strict for this new gifted pilot project that a full three grades had to be scoured before thirty qualified students could be found. Instead of just a class of sixth-graders starting out the program, the founders felt the need to pick the cream of the crop from grades four, five and six. The thirty of us in Miss Privet's class spanned three different years. The first year, there had only been a small number of sixth graders anyway, and when most of us moved up a grade and returned for this, our second year (again with Miss Privet), there was a fresh intake of minuscule fourth graders to take their place.*

This democratisation of the normal grade hierarchy effectively blurred many of the distinctions normally present in the escalating grades as we approached junior high. And to a point, we were all equal, despite ranging in age from an especially young eight (Dale Rowan, who cried all the time and smelled funny) to a nearly pubescent 12 (our beloved Dagmar Hewson-Hill, who had started school late due to a minor diplomat father waiting for his appointed government to fall so his daughter could go to an American school rather than a Somali one). But democracy is rule of the majority, and that first year there was a plurality of fifth graders (14) with an easily cajoled coalition government in the second-in-command fourth graders (nine), leaving the sixth graders (seven) to talk amongst themselves.

Both Jasper Wheeler and Dagmar Hewson-Hill had been fifth graders the first year of the gifted class. Dagmar was our tallest student, but not to the point where she required ostracization. Jasper was of average height, but his braininess and alarmingly mature ego marked him out as her natural opposition. But rather than battle for supremacy over the entire class (excluding the ineffective sixth graders that first year), they instead felt forced to rally their own support.

Dagmar was bright, teacher-pleasing, demonstrably intelligent. She naturally attracted acolytes from the rest of us. Jasper, meanwhile, wore black every day, even at

11, felt himself smarter than Miss Privet, and took an immediate hatred to Dagmar Hewson-Hill. He also, naturally, attracted his own acolytes – Laura Mariotti, for example, his main deputy. The first day of the first year of our class, Dagmar thought she spotted a potential friend in Laura and based a friendship offering on an account of the novels of Judy Blume.

'They speak to me as a young woman,' Dagmar said. 'They talk about things you can't say to your parents. Menstruation –' ('I actually used the word menstruation,' Dagmar told us later. 'I would have hated me, too.') '– and real issues concerning girls our age. There's even one that talks about nocturnal emissions in boys, which I'm not quite sure about, but it was fascinating.'

Laura remained silent through Dagmar's lecture, then said, 'Yeah, I read all those last year. I only read Stephen King and Dune *now. Judy Blume is for insecure whiners who know nothing about the world.'*

Rude, right to her face, just like that. No preamble, no pretence of friendship, just rude, immediately. We did not (and do not) understand that kind of attitude, especially when there were so few of us against the hostility of a larger school of hundreds. But Dagmar's experience was not unique. David Middleton was the one in our group (there's always one) who liked ballet and dressing up and once referred to one of Miss Privet's shirts as a 'blouse'. Derek Bartlett, who claimed to not only smoke cigarettes but could tell the differences in brands, refused to call David anything but 'faggothands'. Linda Zhang was taunted as an 'ignorant sky-god lover' for mentioning The Chronicles of Narnia *to Rainer*

Schlossberg, a friend of Jasper's from their first school together. Tom Hulver, the closest our group got to an athlete, got into the first fight of his life when Neil Corbett threw a basketball at his face during a game of slaughterball in P.E.

Within a month of that first year, lines were drawn. We were part of Dagmar's group. They were part of Jasper's. As we neared the culmination of our second year together, the separation remained. This would prove to have consequences that we naturally now wish we could have predicted.

'WITH ALL DUE RESPECT, MISS PRIVET,' said Jasper Wheeler, leaning back in his seat the day after both groups finished the first phase of digging and burying, 'do we really need yet another set of lectures on how to use a shovel?'

'It's more than just using a shovel, Jasper,' Miss Privet said from the blackboard. 'There are ways of digging so you don't damage your artefacts in the act of uncovering them.'

'Yes, I know that, *Miss Privet*,' Jasper affected the air of someone trying very hard not to lose his patience with a small child, 'and you've taught us how to use those techniques already over several *weeks* of lessons –'

'Retrieval is an entirely different process,' spoke up Dagmar, eyebrows creased in defense.

'Yes, Doggy,' said Jasper, 'thank you for your contribution.'

'It's *Dagmar*,' she hissed.

'I'm sure it is,' said Jasper. 'My point, before *Dag Mar* interrupted me, was that you already went over the process of the delicate and sublime retrieval of artefacts when we watched the video on Tutankhamen.'

'Did we?' Miss Privet seemed to genuinely ask.

'Yes,' said Jasper, flatly, 'and it was very illuminating. It is, perhaps, less illuminating now.'

'Don't talk to Miss Privet that way!' snapped Dagmar.

'*Don't talk to Miss Privet that way,*' Jasper mimicked. 'As a grown woman, I'm sure Miss Privet is capable of fending off a verbal riposte from an eleven-year-old boy.'

'Show off.'

'Suck-up.'

'Children, please.' Miss Privet had promised never to address us as 'children'. 'I know you're eager to get on with things, but I just wanted to re-emphasise how important it is that you don't destroy what you're trying to uncover. Imagine how you would feel if your fellow classmates, in their excitement about digging, destroyed an artefact that you yourself had worked very hard to create.'

'It would serve them right,' said Jasper.

'They'd deserve to lose,' said Dagmar.

'Well,' said Miss Privet, 'there we have it then.'

ON THE FIRST DAY OF *the assignment, camped at the far end of the classroom from Jasper Wheeler, and after our group, based on Dagmar's own idea, had whispered our equal society into being –*

('Miss Privet'll love it,' said David Middleton.

'She'll probably cry again,' said Linda Zhang.

'Remember when she cried over your poem, Pratip?' said Tom Hulver. 'What was it? "U.S. Spells Us" or something?'

'*She cries over* everything,' *said Pratip.*

'*She's definitely going to cry over this,*' *Dagmar said.)*
– we set to work on the nuts and bolts. Chris Tyler and Pola (not Paula) Armstrong were the top artists in our group, though of completely different styles: Chris preferred cartoon dragons and satirical caricatures; Paula was devoted to shadowy silhouettes of unicorns and environmental disasters. Somehow, they pooled their resources, and we began with some very strange sketches of early ideas for artefacts that would reflect absolute equality for everyone. A symbol was our breakthrough. Chris designed one that looked like two orcas chasing each other in a circle. Only later, when all circumstances became as they are, did Chris own up that he had merely stolen a yin and yang symbol from a tattoo on the arm of the uncle he was never supposed to talk to alone. None of the rest of us were old enough to recognise it.

From the symbol flowed everything else: Pola designed coins we could make (from aluminium foil and paper) that had scales as their main motif. She also drew an early sketch for a mosaic she would end up painting herself that emphasized equality and democracy in various ways: a senate made up of equal representation from all parts of society, a map of the main city that had equal buildings in equal-sized sectors, an alternating rota of kings and queens, et cetera.

David Middleton outdid himself creating an entire alphabet based on letters made up of identical halves. Dagmar assigned him to make the required Rosetta stone so that the other group could decipher our (also required) manuscripts of laws and proclamations. Miss

Privet gave us crinkly yellow paper to use for these, and David and Linda Zhang spent days perfecting the final versions.

Everyone contributed something. There were those of us who made papier-mâché weighing scales intended to be theological idols. Some of us sewed sashes for the annually rotating king and queen of our equal society (what with the presence of Dagmar, none of us thought to question the idea of a thoroughly equal democracy having a monarch). Others built a chariot from reinforced construction paper and balsa wood that was intended to be the main religious artefact symbolising the journey of the civilization's gods between the equivalently worshiped sun and moon.

Even with our gifted status, it was very difficult not to grow bored with such a patently bland over-riding theme, but we remembered how disappointed Miss Privet had been at the collapse of the recent Equal Rights Amendment; she had mentioned it several times with what we sincerely hoped was only temporary bitterness. We knew our society would please her. Our parents, too, would no doubt receive glowing reports at parent-teacher conferences about how children like us, with our generously humanitarian outlook, were the real hope for the future, that there was much in our flawless characters for our families to be proud of as we were clearly future leaders of this country.

Many of us, if you were able to ask us now (but you can't, you can't), would remember it as a very lonely time.

* * *

235

WE WERE MORE EAGER FOR Phase 2 than we had been for Phase 1. At last we could find out what Jasper Wheeler and his minions had been up to for the past weeks. Group B took our needly glade of pine trees, and we took over their scoop of earth at the base of the short hill. It was cloudy but not rainy (as it often is in Tacoma) and surprisingly warm, even for spring. The air felt wet, hot and heavy, the sweat of a nap that has gone on too long. We again had our shovels and spades, brushes and spoons. Pratip was once again enlisted to string a criss-cross pattern of quadrants along the border of Group B's area. We were to name these (A1, A2, etc) and detail the exact layout of where and at what orientation we found each of Group B's artefacts. Just like real archeologists.

Miss Privet, who spent the day disappearing from our consciousnesses, left us to it.

Again without consulting any of the rest of the group, we were dressed almost identically. We all wore khaki shorts, even though shorts were not technically allowed in the school's dress code. We all had the same suede boots, some of which had obviously been purchased the night before but none of which had ever been discussed. We all wore painter hats as well; true, it was a briefly-lived fashion statement in the early 80s, but no one among us had owned one before today. The feeling, if any of us had asked, was that they were the closest we could each come to a proper sun visor. But we did not ask. We merely knew. As Group A, we looked like a specially organised team of professional diggers.

'I found a knife,' said David Middleton, almost making it a question.

'A real knife?' said Richie Goldstein.

'Can't be,' said Dagmar. 'There's no way that's allowed.'

'It's real, all right,' said David.

'But that's . . .' said Dagmar, looking irked and confused. 'That can't be right. How is that an artefact? How is that creating anything? We were supposed to *make* everything. You can't just stick a knife in the ground and call it an artefact.'

'Maybe it's part of something,' said Tom Hulver. 'Keep digging. Maybe it's part of a set.'

'Miss Privet wouldn't have let them just bury a knife,' said Linda Zhang.

'Would she?' said Terry Yotter.

'No,' said Dagmar. 'Keep digging.'

'Here's another knife,' said David Middleton. 'And another. And . . . *Oh*, I see. Look.'

We looked. The knives, which seemed to be just ordinary steak knives with painted handles, were arranged in a circle, points inward, a radiating sun of knives.

'What's that in the middle?' asked Larry Patmos.

David Middleton brushed away the surrounding loose dirt. 'It's a little person. A little carved person.'

'What's that supposed to be?' asked Pola Armstrong.

'Who knows?' said Dagmar, scornfully. 'Probably something stupid like a torture device, knowing Jasper. Just mark down how we found it. We'll figure it out later.'

'I found their mosaic!' called Chris Tyler from a far corner.

We gathered around him as he uncovered it, blowing the dirt away from the paint with light puffs from his mouth. 'Wow,' he said.

'You've got to be kidding,' said Tom Hulver.

'How did Miss Privet let them get away with *that*?' asked Linda Zhang.

'Pathetic,' spat Dagmar, scowling at the mosaic. 'Pathetic and childish and stupid. It was obviously a waste of time to care so much about our civilization if that's all Group B was doing.' She made a scoffing sound and shook her head, summoning up her worst insult. 'Immature,' she said, 'just so immature.'

THAT WAS NOT THE FIRST *time we had been pitted against Jasper Wheeler's group. The year before, the class had gone through another major scientific project designed to be fun and challenging to gluttonous minds. That time, the subject had been geology, and in a remarkable reflection of the early Reagan years, each group pretended to be an oil company searching for suitable drilling sites on a made-up continent. The continent – called, as all fictional continents seem to be, Atlantia – only existed on the green computer screen of an Apple IIe. Divided up into sectors with different monochrome patterns representing different terrains and geological conditions, we had 180 different squares from which to select oil drilling sites, a very few of which would produce gushers (of 100 million barrels), others lesser levels of oil production, and still others providing nothing at all. The challenge was that we were only allowed to select five different squares in total, so we had to base our decisions on careful research.*

Using Apple-provided workbooks, we learned how oil was created (though 'dead dinosaurs' was the only bit of the complicated process that sticks with us now), the different kinds of rocks that trapped it (shales and . . . other rocks that also managed to be easily forgettable), and how oil companies did years of research before drilling in specific sites to 'maximise the saving of the environment while providing clean and efficient fuel for the convenient use of everyone'. We were to take the knowledge gleaned from the corporate workbooks, study our map of Atlantia, perform computerised tests, analyse the results, and then decide on potential drilling sites.

Though there were minor variances because of the slightly different batches of students in the successive years, the two oil-drilling groups were essentially the same as the archeology teams. The Carbonites were headed by Dagmar Hewson-Hill. Texxon, Inc. by Jasper Wheeler. The project had added frisson in that we were in direct competition. Whichever side found the most oil in their five drilling sites would win a pizza lunch while the other group would be stuck with their normal brown bags.

The drilling took place on the project's final day. After all our research and tests, each group had drawn up lists of preferred squares with lists of alternates should the other group duplicate one of the choices. Higher aggregate scores on various geology pop quizzes allowed Jasper and Texxon, Inc. to make the first selection. The

He was placed ceremonially at the front of the class, so that both groups could see the success (or not) of the alternate drillings. Jasper Wheeler walked up to the front with a smirk on his face.

'P, 9,' he said, typing in the coordinates. There were brief quizzical looks within our group. P9 was nowhere on our list of possible sites. Could we have missed something? The computer took a dramatic pause as an oil well was painstakingly constructed onscreen, then a shout of joy from Texxon, Inc., as drops of oil shot from the top of the well.

'15 million barrels,' said Miss Privet. 'Not bad.'

Jasper looked annoyed. 'It should have been a gusher.'

'15 million barrels isn't bad, Jasper,' Miss Privet repeated. 'Dagmar, would you like to take your turn?'

Dagmar went up to the computer looking like a vet regretfully having to put a brave horse to sleep. 'C, 3,' she said.

'C3?' Jasper said, an incredulous look on his face.

'That's what I said.'

Again the oil well constructed itself. The pause seemed even longer this time, then the screen turned bright green and the word 'GUSHER!' blinked off and on in all caps. Jubilant cheers arose from us in the Carbonites. Miss Privet clapped. 'Well done,' she said. 'Very well done. Congratulations.'

'Something's wrong, Miss Privet,' said Jasper. 'C3 shouldn't have had anything.'

'Nothing's wrong, Jasper.' Miss Privet's voice was tender, gentle even. 'Except maybe your calculations.'

'Miss Privet –'

'Please have someone from your group take your next turn, Jasper.'

Jasper Wheeler stared at her. A quick flick of his head sent up Laura Mariotti. She typed in D1, again not on our list over in the Carbonities. She received 25 million barrels, not bad, but nowhere close to our 100-million-barrel gusher. Tom Hulver went up next for our group. The same pause, the same all caps announcement. After two turns, Texxon, Inc. had 35 million barrels. The Carbonites had 200 million barrels. The rout was on. By the end, we had hit four gushers out of five and received 50 million barrels for the one non-gusher. Through whatever miscalculation was permeating their statistics, Jasper Wheeler's group ended up with just 85 million barrels total. We won on our first turn.

'Something's not right, Miss Privet,' an angry Jasper said as our celebration raged. 'Our calculations –'

'Must have been off,' Miss Privet said. 'I've checked this program over, Jasper. There's nothing wrong with it. I told you you should have done more tests.'

'We did plenty of tests.'

'But the Carbonites did more.'

'Miss Privet, I really don't see –'

'You lost, Jasper. I know you're disappointed, but one of life's big lessons is learning how to be gracious when you've been beaten fair and square.'

'I don't think it was fair and square –'

'That's enough, Jasper.' Miss Privet gave him her 'that's enough' smile. 'It's how life goes sometimes.'

'We'll share our pizza with you,' Dagmar cut in. 'We

*always intended to all along. It wouldn't be any fun
watching you guys not have any.'*

Jasper's lips pursed, his nostrils inflating. Dagmar's
face gave nothing away, but her gaze held his.

'Now, isn't that nice, Jasper?' said Miss Privet.
'Everyone wins. Shouldn't you say "thank you" on
behalf of your group?'

Jasper's voice was cold enough to cut through our
victorious chatter. 'Thank you, Dagmar, and congratu-
lations,' he said, the temperature in the room dropping.
'May you get all that you deserve.'

'So FAR, ALL IT SEEMS to be is something about time,
maybe time *travel*, and something about human sacri-
fice,' said Terry Yotter.

Dagmar rolled her eyes. 'Oh, my gosh, how
completely immature.'

Dagmar had been seething ever since Phase 2 digging
was stopped by Miss Privet. Not only did all of Group
B's artefacts centre around bloodletting and an obses-
sion with clocks, we hadn't found their Rosetta Stone,
leaving us unable to decipher any of their laws and
manuscripts and forcing us to guess about most of their
society. This was in the rules. Miss Privet had allegedly
supervised burial of the required parts of the project
(though she was nowhere to be found when we buried
our own Rosetta Stone), and therefore, if we missed
anything important, it was our own fault.

'Real archeologists don't have a map,' she told a
steaming Dagmar. 'Look at it as a bigger challenge. I
know you're up to it.'

This encouraging compliment, normally the *ne plus ultra* of our gifted existence, only served to make Dagmar angrier. She returned to our working-half of the class-room.

'He didn't bury it,' she whispered angrily. 'I'm sure of it. Either that, or he broke the rules and buried it too deep or outside of their area.'

'We dug everywhere,' said Richie Goldstein.

'Yes,' said Dagmar, 'we did.' She punched Tom Hulver on the shoulder.

'Ow.'

'Don't be a baby.'

'Well, we're gonna have to come up with *something*,' said Linda Zhang, whose anxiety over potentially getting less than an A was starting to tell.

'Like I said.' Terry Yotter gestured exasperatedly at the mosaic, the dirty piles of papier-mâché clocks, the bewildering assortment of knives. 'It's time or time travel or something stupid like that.'

'And the mosaic,' started Chris Tyler.

'The mosaic should get them flunked,' spat Dagmar.

The mosaic was a hallucinatory, *Grand Guignol* night-mare. Either Jasper or Dale Chalmers, his main artist, must have found a Hieronymus Bosch print somewhere – Bosch and Dali being the two patron artistic saints of the gifted child – and ran with it. The mosaic was littered with small figures, most in the process of disembowel-ment or decapitation or flaying or immolation or infan-ticide or drowning or defenestration or any one of a number of deaths. Upon closer examination, it got worse. Each murder seemed to be perpetrated by the same man dressed in black upon the same woman dressed in white. The man looked a lot like Jasper, and the woman looked a lot like Dagmar.

'I *think* you may be reading a bit more into it than is really there,' said Miss Privet to a further outraged Dagmar. 'Lots of older societies were fairly brutal, and some of them even seemed to have the kinds of massacres shown here.' Her smile was anodyne. 'It's not my cup of tea, but you guys need free rein to your imaginations.'

The outer edge of the mosaic was painted with clocks which, when read clockwise, seemed to be moving backwards in time. At the centre of the mosaic was a single larger version of the Jasper figure holding a knife over the prone Dagmar figure. He was more priest-like in this pose and seemed to be praying.

'Maybe he can go back in time so he gets to kill her over and over again,' said David Middleton.

'Shut up, David,' said Dagmar.

'Are you getting taller, David?' asked Terry Yotter, out of the blue.

David shrugged. 'I don't think so. Maybe.'

'It's just . . . you used to look shorter compared to Dagmar than you do.'

We all glanced over at them to look. To our surprise –

'*Equality?*' Jasper's taunting voice broke in. He stood just outside our work area. '*That's* your theme? Equality?'

'You're not supposed to be over here, Jasper,' said Tom Hulver.

'Well, I'm bored,' said Jasper. 'Your civilization was

so pathetically easy to figure out, we have an amazing amount of time left over.'

'Go away, Jasper,' said Dagmar.

'And *equality*.' He stressed the word, as if it was something distasteful. 'Of all the predictable, simpering, soft-headed things you could have picked. *Equality*.'

'It's better than some stupid, childish thing about human sacrifice and mass death,' Dagmar said. 'I mean, *come on*, Jasper, how predictable could you be. *Yawn*, this is me *yawning*.'

'You do realise of course that all equality really means is that you're as weak as your weakest member.' He looked at David. 'Which would probably be you, faggothands.'

'Miss Privet!' called Dagmar.

Jasper changed tactic as Miss Privet got up from her desk. 'How are you coming along with ours?'

'You cheated,' said Dagmar. 'You didn't bury your Rosetta Stone.'

'Oh, yes, we did,' said Jasper. 'You just didn't find it.'

'Jasper, come away from there now,' said Miss Privet.

Jasper laughed as he returned to his group. 'And that's not the only thing you didn't find,' he said, just loud enough for us to hear.

WE MIGHT HAVE BEEN MORE, *once. There was an attempted defection, early in the second year. Marlon Lerner, an extremely portly new pupil with a crewcut, who prided himself on reading British science fiction and who religiously played Advanced Dungeons &*

Dragons (to the point of having lead figures and wooden dice, even the four-sided one), had taken the gothic seriousness of Jasper Wheeler's group as something he could fit his heretofore shameful manias into. Unfortunately for Marlon, all that was lacking in Jasper Wheeler's group at the time was a scapegoat, a whipping boy to be the target of their leader's insults. These were fairly typical to begin with: 'Prepare for an earthquake, Marlon's about to run' or 'Are you going to have two birthday cakes, Marlon? One for you and one for your guests?' Jasper Wheeler's group would laugh. Marlon would laugh along, too. Even some of our group, overhearing, laughed at a joke at the expense of someone besides ourselves.

But then Jasper started to take a particular avenue: 'How long has it been since you've actually seen your penis, Marlon?' 'Are you sure you even have a penis? Are you sure you're not a girl underneath all that flab?' 'You've got breasts, Marlon, maybe you should start wearing a bra.' We would hear these comments underneath the rusted monkey bars where our class was forced to take refuge each recess. There was little room for the two groups to separate, but we did our best. The taunting, though, remained audible to all. 'When you play AD&D, are you a sorceress? An Amazon? A witch?'

Marlon would try to laugh, but we watched him falter as the days went on. 'Do you think a nice man would ever want a fat wife like you, Marlon?' 'Has your mother talked to you about period pains yet, Marlon?' 'How do you know what you're feeling down there isn't just a flap of your maturing vagina, Marlon?'

It surprised no one in our group when Marlon started talking to David Middleton, who played AD&D himself. First in class, then in the more important monkey bars, Marlon began to spend time huddled with David, even on occasion laughing in a manner that was other than self-inflicted. We, not excluding Marlon, waited with some anxiety to see what, if anything, Jasper would do in response to this rejection of his side of the class. Seven days passed. Ten. Marlon became a regular feature in our group, though tending to stick mainly with David out of shyness.

Then one recess, just as we were all reaching the point of forgetting that Marlon had ever been anything but one of us, Jasper brought out an instant camera.

'Look what I got for Christmas,' he announced, though it was only early October. He flashed a picture immediately, a print of surprised-looking members of his group fading into view moments later on the celluloid-backed slip of cardboard the camera spat out. Even our group was curious, watching Jasper snap photos of his friends and disciples. He kept looking over at us, his face smug.

'Hey, Marlon,' he called.

Marlon, doing his best to look small against the edge of the monkey bars, said, 'What?'

'I think maybe we can help you out.'

'Help me out how?'

'Prove once and for all whether you're a girl or a boy.'

'Fuck off, Jasper,' said Marlon, afraid, and the air positively crackled at his words. You could hear our

collective intake of breath even on the noisy playground. Gifteds, raised in good homes, were above such profanity.

'What did you say, Marlon?' Jasper said, coming closer.

'Leave me alone.'

'Leave him, Jasper,' said Tom Hulver.

'Shut up, Tom,' said Jasper. 'I do believe this fat little piggy told me to eff off. Which is not something I think I can tolerate.' Jasper nodded, giving some kind of signal. Derek Bartlett and Rainer Schlossberg, his two largest henchmen, moved forward and grabbed Marlon by either arm.

'Now we're going to find out once and for all if this fat, disgusting slob of a thing . . .' He lightly smacked Marlon's cheeks. '. . . is a boy or a girl.' He grabbed the buckle of Marlon's belt and started undoing it. Marlon struggled, his body thrashing, but Jasper landed a fist in his stomach. The violence shocked us all. Marlon went through the rest of his ordeal in a terrified and terrifying quiet acquiescence. Jasper undid Marlon's fly and pulled his pants down to his knees, then grabbed his underwear and yanked them down.

We did nothing to stop this. We still do not know why.

Jasper knelt with his camera and aimed it at Marlon's penis, a penis we all saw right there, pink and small and hairless, exposed in broad daylight on our own playground. Because we could be assumed to take care of ourselves, we were a blind spot on the playground monitor's radar. The other kids, having won our exile to the monkey bars, ignored us. We were Marlon's only possible defense, but we had turned somehow into merely his witnesses.

Even with the bright overcast, the camera flashed when the picture was taken. Marlon flinched at the light burst, then we saw yellow liquid flow from the small bit of flesh that we all knew we should never have seen. Rainer and Derek held Marlon until he stopped wetting himself. By then, the picture had developed, and Jasper turned it to Marlon's face, now a mess of tears and snot.

'What do you know?' Jasper said. 'She's got a dick after all.' He slid the picture into his pocket and turned his back. Rainer and Derek let go of Marlon. An empty zone appeared around him. He pulled up his soggy underpants and trousers, his chin trembling. Dagmar took the first step towards him.

'Marlon –'

'Don't tell anyone,' he said fiercely, almost hysterically.

'But Miss Privet should –'

'Don't tell anyone!'

'But –'

'Please,' he said, looking at all of us. 'Please.'

It was something we would naturally have done, tell Miss Privet. We were exactly the sort of children who would go running to her in an instant to report the wrongdoing of a classmate. But as Marlon Lerner tried to brush the urine on his trousers to get it to dry, we agreed to his request out of shame that none of us had tried to help him, that not one of us had intervened to prevent this unimaginable recess. We were silent out of our own guilt, out of the chance that we might get into trouble too. Which was unthinkable.

Marlon Lerner attended classes for another week or so, a pariah from both groups, until his unhappiness was so obvious that his parents took him out of the gifted program, deciding that he must have missed his friends from his old school, friends that we all knew from our own experience did not exist.

'BUT MISS PRIVET, HE SAID we didn't find everything.'

'Dagmar, you know the rules. Each group had the same amount of allotted time to find what they could. Real archeologists don't even know what they're looking for and have to recreate civilizations from less than what you've found.'

Dagmar took a deep breath, preparing the argument that went against everything our group believed about itself. It was necessary, though, and we supported this tactical surrender.

'But we're *not* archeologists, Miss Privet,' she said, through regretful clenched teeth.

'Dagmar –'

'We're students. We're –' Dagmar gulped, '– little kids. Jasper's group buried his Rosetta Stone too well. There wasn't enough time for us to find it.'

'His group found yours.'

'That's because we played by the rules,' Dagmar could not keep herself from saying.

'Miss Privet,' Jasper Wheeler walked into the conversation. 'It *is* possible that my group did bury the Rosetta

Stone a bit too deep. Out of sheer enthusiasm for this brilliant project, I assure you.'

'Jasper –' Miss Privet started.

'We intended no deception,' Jasper continued, smiling warmly at Dagmar. 'If we did go overboard, it really is only fair to let Dagmar's group return to the site for a bit more digging. Who knows? There might even be more things to be found.'

Miss Privet looked skeptical. 'If you went outside the rules of burial, Jasper –'

'Not intentionally.'

'Yeah, right,' Dagmar said.

'I assure you,' said Jasper. 'Perhaps we just had stronger diggers. I'm not sure David Middleton is as good with a spade as Rainer Schlossberg, as a purely random example. It seems only fair to give them a bit more time.'

Dagmar, in a heroic action as she was forced to perform it in front of Jasper, played our trump card. 'It's making us feel bad about ourselves, Miss Privet.'

'Oh, Dagmar,' Miss Privet said, her body slumping in sympathy. 'Of course, then. But I can really only give you one more hour. You'll have to use the lunchtime recess period so you don't miss any of today's lessons. Is that okay?'

'Thank you, Miss Privet.'

'Don't I get any thanks?' said Jasper.

Dagmar turned her back on him.

'That's okay,' he called to her. 'You can thank me later.'

It was still humid. We were already sweating when we reached the site at lunchtime.

'Stupid Jasper,' Dagmar mumbled to herself as her

shovel went into the dirt. 'Stupid cheater,' she said. 'Stupid damn child.'

Our clothes were once again similar. The khaki shorts were the same, but now even the blue shirts were less varied. We all wore light-blue button-front Oxfords, which some of us, if pressed, would not have even remembered owning. Our shoes were the same light suede boots. Our hair had taken on a shaggy uniformity from group-member to group-member. Even our heights, from a certain angle, seemed to conform to a group average. We dug in an unconscious rhythm, as if the same silent metronome were clicking in all of us. If any of us had noticed, we might have been alarmed. But no one did, and so we were not.

'Found something!' called Tom Hulver.

'Is it the damn Rosetta Stone?' said Dagmar.

'You're sure swearing a lot,' said Pratip Mukherji.

'Shut up,' Dagmar said. 'Tom, is it the Stone or isn't it?'

Tom said nothing for a moment, using a brush to whisk away the dirt. What slowly appeared seemed almost to be –

'Fur?' said David Middleton.

Linda Zhang looked alarmed. 'They didn't kill an animal, did they?'

'No,' said Tom, brushing more dirt away. 'It looks like a wig.'

'Oh, for heaven's sake,' said Dagmar. 'They probably buried a dummy's head just in case we were too stupid to figure out the human sacrifice thing.'

'It's not a dummy's head.' There was something taut in Tom's voice. 'The smell.' He covered his mouth and nose with one hand. We all caught the odor he meant, a vomitingly sweet smell of milk and raw meat gone very bad. Terry Yotter started to retch.

'Of course, it's a dummy's head,' said Dagmar.

'How would they get a dummy's head to rot?' asked Larry Patmos.

'I don't know,' said Dagmar, 'pack it with fruit or hamburger or something.'

She grabbed the brush from Tom and went over to the spot. Trying to hold her breath, letting out gasps from between locked lips, she brushed away the dirt, gradually working her way down from the crown of the head. 'Jasper, you little shithead,' she muttered.

She brushed and brushed, not wanting to damage whatever it was buried in the dirt, doing her best to ignore the smell. When she finally managed to brush the face clear, there was silence. Even Dagmar's breathing stopped. We stared at the thing that sat in a little hollow in Group B's burial pit.

'What is it?' whispered Linda Zhang.

There were several gashes across its face, and blood – it *looked* like blood – had hardened into brown clumps across the eyes and nose. The blood could have been faked, even a lifelike rubbery head could have been made somehow, somewhere, but there was something about the bruising, something about the tint of the swollen flesh, something about its expression that made it seem impossibly real. Even through the gashes, even through the slight decomposition, we recognised the face. The wiry hair, anyway, was unmistakable.

'It's Miss Privet,' said Dagmar.

WE REMEMBER SOMETHING THAT ONLY *makes sense now,
in retrospect. We remember it, so it must be part of our
story.*

*Near the end of the previous school year, after the
oil-drilling project, Miss Privet tried to heal the rift in
our classroom by bringing in her pet guinea pigs, Gloria
and Helen (after two of her personal heroes, she told us
wistfully), for us to feed, play with and get peed on by
in the weeks leading up to summer break. Gloria was
brown on top with a white tummy, Helen nearly all
black with brown tufts along her bottom ridge. They
were so furry they hardly registered as animals. Their
eyes, mouths and feet were obscured by fur, and it was
only possible to know which end was which by a tenta-
tive nose that seemed their only link with the world.
Feeding rights were much fought over, so Miss Privet
set up a timetable and allowed us to play with them in
small groups.*

'Don't get grabby,' she said. 'They can get very don't
drop them!'

*'I wasn't, Miss Privet,' said Jasper Wheeler. 'I was
holding up Gloria here to look underneath.'*

*'That's Helen,' Miss Privet said, 'and you be careful
with her, Jasper. I've had them for a long time. They're
very precious to me.'*

*Jasper shrugged. 'Nothing to see anyway. Just more
fur.'*

*'Look, Miss Privet,' said Dagmar. 'Gloria's asleep on
my lap.'*

'That's very sweet.'

Eventually and perhaps inevitably, there came the moment when, during guinea pig playtime, Miss Privet was called away to the principal's office.

'You're all mature enough to treat Gloria and Helen right, okay?' she said on leaving. 'I'm counting on you.'

'Yes, Miss Privet,' both Jasper and Dagmar said.

Jasper waited until the door closed. He turned to his friends. 'Wanna see something?'

'What are you going to do, Jasper?' asked Dagmar, alarmed.

'Mind your own business for once, eh, Doggy?' He took Helen from her cage and carried her to the art table. The art table was covered in various rainbows of construction paper, glues, rulers, scissors, glitter, the standard grade school complement. It was also home to the paper cutter, a flat board with a handle raised from one end that held a curved blade along its edge. The motion of bringing down the large metal handle to slice thick stacks of paper was almost erotically satisfying, and we manufactured reasons to do so during art hour. Jasper headed straight for it.

'Jasper!' called Dagmar.

'I just want to show you all something,' he said, his voice light. Dagmar stepped forward, but Jasper was too fast, too fluid. He placed Helen under the blade and brought it down with an authoritative whunk. Several of us screamed. Jasper had cut Helen completely in half. He held up a tail end and a nose end in either hand, blood and viscera dripping onto the floor. Terry Yotter was sick into a garbage can. Even Jasper's group looked ashen. Jasper himself just smiled, blood dripping down his arms.

The door flew open, no doubt in response to the screams. We turned to see Miss Privet bounding through, a look of ferocious protection on her face. 'What? What?! What is it?'

Dagmar tried to talk through traumatized tears. 'Jasper . . .' she gasped. 'He . . .' She turned to point. We all turned. Jasper held a sleepy-looking but very much whole Helen in one hand, scratching her behind the ears with the other. Helen leaned into his fingers for a better position. There was no blood on Jasper's hands, none on the floor, none on Helen. No trace at all of what we had seen with our own eyes.

'What?' said Jasper, innocent as a new-born babe. 'What'd I do?'

We believed we had been tricked, that Jasper had grossed us out, fooled us with some textbook magic. We realise now that this perhaps is the one important thing we had missed.

MISS PRIVET DECLINED TO RUN to the dig site, settling for a quick walk behind our group as we tried to pull her along with our frantic gravity. Her pace indicated she was taking this seriously but was not about to be made to look ridiculous if this was more of Jasper's tomfoolery. She had refused to end her lunch hour early, saying it was nothing that could not wait until after her three-bean salad, but then at the start of the afternoon session, she confined Jasper's group to the classroom and followed us out. We could read concern in her actions, but we also saw a desire to keep control of things. We regarded this as fair enough.

Her composure lasted until she saw her own head sticking up from the ground, partially decomposed with the terrible gashes on its face. She dropped to one knee in front of it. We waited for her to speak. And waited some more.

'What is this?' she finally said.

'Some trick of Jasper's, we think,' said Dagmar.

Miss Privet sat back on her haunches. 'It looks so real.'

'He needs help, Miss Privet,' Dagmar said. 'A psychiatrist or something. I mean, really.'

'I think you may be right, Dagmar.' Miss Privet reached forward to touch it, her nose wrinkling at the smell. She pressed the skin on the thing's temple. Her fingers left a dent, and a gel-like substance came out of the closed eye. Miss Privet shuddered, genuinely shuddered.

'Is it just a head?' she asked.

We looked from one to another. 'What do you mean?' asked Dagmar.

'Is there more underneath? A body?' She said, as if to herself, 'No, there couldn't be. Could there?' She reached out a hand to Dagmar. 'Give me your shovel.'

We watched as she dug around the head, revealing a neck, shoulders, then an upper body. If it *was* a corpse, it had been buried vertically.

'Look,' said Tom Hulver. 'It's the same shirt.'

The body, Miss Privet, whatever it was, was wearing the same shirt as the real live Miss Privet standing over it, the same floral pattern, the same missing top button, the same three-bean salad dressing stain on the left front pocket.

'But I just got that stain today,' said Miss Privet. 'How could –'

'Miss Privet!' yelled Chris Tyler, working at some loose soil in the corner of the plot. He scooped dirt with his hands. Another tuft of hair, soon another head, another face, Linda Zhang's. 'And another,' said Chris, pushing away more dirt. Next to Linda, also buried vertically, was Terry Yotter, the same gashes on his face and forehead, his jaw torn away almost completely.

More furious digging by us and Miss Privet uncovered the heads and shoulders of every member of Group A: Pratip Mukherji and Tom Hulver, Richie Goldstein and Pola Armstrong, Larry Patmos and Chris Tyler, David Middleton and Robbie Normer, and the rest of us. And Dagmar Hewson-Hill, too, of course, sliced up in a way unbearable to look at. We stood over our own corpses, which all wore the same clothes we had on our living backs.

'Miss Privet?' said Dagmar.

'I don't know, Dagmar,' said Miss Privet. 'I just don't know.'

'Which, I must say, Miss Privet,' said Jasper Wheeler, 'is not at all surprising.'

When we looked up at the sound of Jasper's voice and saw Group B surrounding us along the edge of the dig site, we realised it was over. They stood above us, shovels and spades and other digging implements suddenly weapons in their hands. Though we also had our own shovels, from our low vantage point in the dug-up hole these suddenly seemed weak and ineffective. Jasper said nothing more as his group raised their armoury.

Our group fought very little. We greeted our deaths with what we saw as mature, adult resignation, a quiet sad dignity, accepting our fates in a way that we imagined would have impressed anyone who saw us. We could not say the same for Miss Privet, who screamed and screamed and screamed.

WHO WERE WE? WE ARE *forgetting, have forgotten. We are ghosts here, who have told this story. It's all we seem to have now, our only remaining gift.*

May we tell it to you again?

Notes and Acknowledgements

Two of the stories in this collection were previously published: 'Sydney Is a City of Jaywalkers' in *Genre* magazine (US), and 'The Way All Trends Do' in *Ambit* (UK). My thanks to the editors of both.

'Jesus' Elbows and Other Christian Urban Myths' contains one urban myth told to me in an email as absolute truth by its sender, whom I'll let remain anonymous (though believers that true are notoriously hard to embarrass). Another is plucked and adapted from the swirling worldwide urban myth ether. The others are invented. I decline to say which.

The epigraph is from the song 'Zebra', from the album *69 Love Songs* by the Magnetic Fields; lyrics written by Stephin Merrit. Copyright © 1999 Stephin Merrit, published by Gay and Loud (ASCAP). Reprinted with permission.

Thanks to: Michelle Kass; Resham Naqvi; Philip Gwyn Jones, Jon Butler, Karen Duffy, Sarah Savitt, and all the other fine folk at Flamingo; T. C. Boyle; Patrick Neate; Nicola Barker (for the Sillitoe!); Jonathan Ruffle for a timely printer lifebuoy; John Mullins, Andrew Thiele, and Phil Rodak. Special thanks to Patrick Gale for his unfailing generosity, and to Patrick again and Aidan Hicks for their hospitality.

And my love to Marc Nowell.